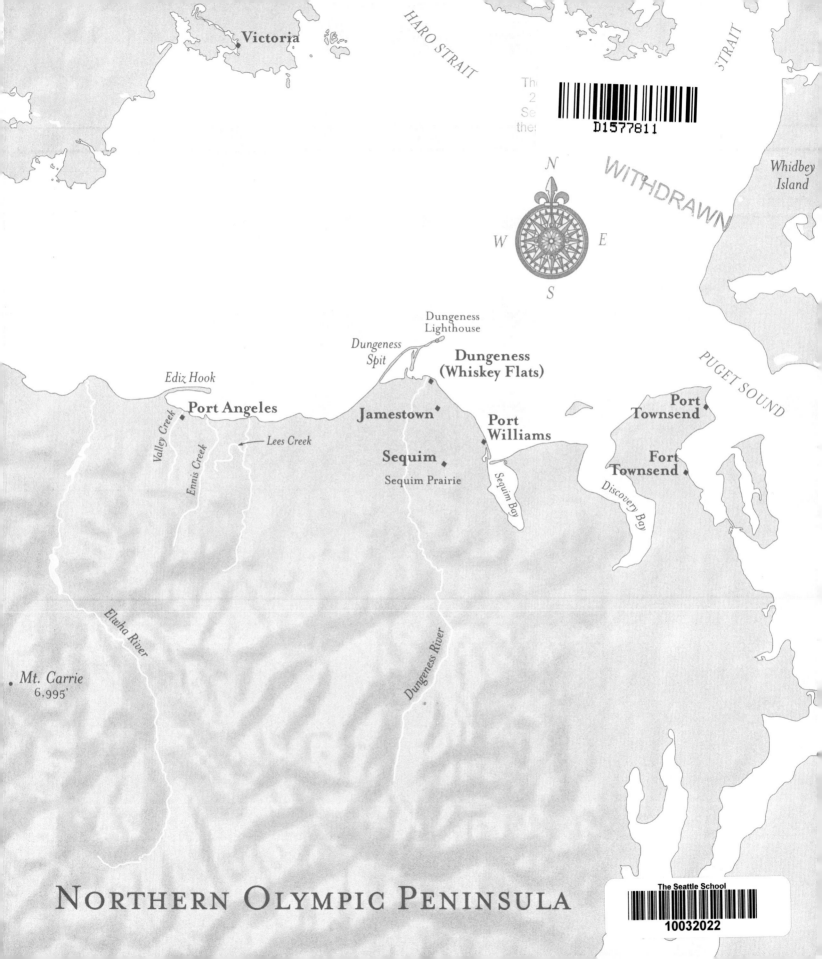

Victoria

HARO STRAIT

STRAIT

Whidbey
Island

N
W   E
S

PUGET SOUND

Dungeness
Lighthouse

Dungeness
Spit

**Dungeness
(Whiskey Flats)**

Ediz Hook

Port Angeles

Jamestown

**Port
Williams**

**Port
Townsend**

Valley Creek

Ennis Creek

Lees Creek

Sequim

Sequim Prairie

Sequim Bay

**Fort
Townsend**

Discovery Bay

• *Mt. Carrie*
6,995'

Elwha River

Dungeness River

NORTHERN OLYMPIC PENINSULA

WOMEN TO RECKON WITH:

UNTAMED WOMEN OF THE OLYMPIC WILDERNESS

Also by Gary Peterson
and Glynda Peterson Schaad

High Divide

WOMEN TO RECKON WITH:

Untamed Women of the Olympic Wilderness

By
Gary Peterson and Glynda Peterson Schaad

PUBLISHED BY POSEIDON PEAK PUBLISHING

First Edition, 2007.
First Printing 2007
Second Printing 2010

Printed by: Everbest Printing Co., Ltd., Nansha, China through **Alaska Print Brokers**, Anchorage, Alaska.

ISBN 978-1-57833-387-5

Published by:
POSEIDON PEAK PUBLISHING
4913 Upper Hoh Road
Forks, Wa 98331

To order: 360-374-5254 or FAX 360-374-5266
Email: poseidonpeak@gmail.com
web: poseidonpeak.com

Book and jacket design: Magdalena Bassett, www.bassettstudio.com
Photo scanning and restoration: DJ Bassett, www.historicphotopreservation.com

Painting "Wreck of the Sv. Nikolai" by Jack Datisman

Photographs:
Peterson Family collection
Olympic National Park
    Fanny Taylor photos
Polly Polhamus collection
Forks Timber Museum
Clallam County Museum
Randy and Cheri Rapp collection
Liane White collection
Cowan collection
Leroy Smith collection
Marian Schumack collection
Beckstead collection
Sharon Nilsen collection
John McNutt collection
Glenn King collection
Lela Mae Morgenroth collection

*With appreciation to Oscar and Wilma Peterson
who instilled in their descendents the pioneer
spirit of their ancestors.*

Outing in the Big Timber.   *Cowan Collection*

Preceding page: Hoh River Homesteaders. 1900.
Leroy Smith Collectiuon

Above: Friends at Lake Crescent. 1900.

Polhamus Collection

INTRODUCTION

Most of the women of this book did not come west to become dutiful housewives of hard-working pioneers. Although they may have all at times fulfilled that role, each had her own vision and made her own choices. Harriet Pullen and her friend, Minerva Troy, headed north to Alaska in 1897 at the peak of the Gold Rush. Caroline Jones homesteaded remote Fairholme at the west end of Lake Crescent. Don't try to find her back trail—it's as cold as the glacier on Mt. Carrie. Anna Petrovna, the Russian castaway "went Native" and lived out her short life as a slave of the Makah. Susie Morgenroth, a Quileute, tried hoquat (white) culture and it didn't agree with her. Martha Maybury rose above bigotry and racism to live a life of benevolence and community service. Laura Peters dreamed of a worker's paradise in Port Angeles.

Most stayed on the good side of the law while pushing the limits of Victorian and post-Victorian society. Some ventured to the dark side. Passion, jealousy, and revenge in copious quantities were ingredients for the brew drunk by the three-timing Wild Rose of Lake Pleasant. The recipe was deadly.

For all their imperfection, the women of this book dreamed big and lived large. They flourished in a land that made them strong, independent, confident, and self-reliant. Even more importantly, they seized opportunity often in the face of great obstacle and therein lies their inspiration for us today.

ACKNOWLEDGEMENTS

Women to Reckon With is a celebration in words and pictures of twelve nineteenth century women who collectively changed the cultural landscape of the North Olympic Peninsula. They are women whose stories have seen only limited circulation.

We are greatly indebted to the descendents of these women who have served as the keepers of the family archives, both in picture and word. Without their generosity this book would not have been possible.

For their pictures and interview time we would like to thank Bob Bowlby, Lincoln Sands, Elizabeth Barlow, Elsie Motler, Glenn King, John Carter, Jacilee Wray, Lela Mae Morgenroth, Liane White, Randy and Cheri Rapp, Wynona M. Ross, Barbara Thompson, Beverly Balch Blair, Maxine Selmer, Helen McCallum, Ron Shearer, Patsy Adams, Jack Datisman, Stan Burrowes, Carol Pacheco, John McNutt, the Tom Rixon family and Marian Schumack.

For technical support we would like to thank the Forks Timber Museum, Francis Kyle, Katie Peterson, Kathy Duncan, Olympic National Park, the Jamestown Library, Stan Peterson, Charlotte Peterson, Amy Pruss and Larry Burtness.

For the book's elegant layout and design we would like to thank Magdalena Bassett, bassettstudio.com. Also critical to the book's appearance were the photo restoration skills of DJ Bassett, historicphotopreservation.com, who electronically teased details from many damaged originals. The editors/authors owe a special debt of gratitude for research and writing to Dona Cloud, June Robinson and Sharon Howe of the Clallam County Historical Society and to the director, Kathy Monds, who generously made available the resources of the Historical Society.

This book's bibliography provided the background information for the text. Of note in this regard are the works of Kenneth N. Owens, George A Pettitt, Jay V. Powell, Jane G. Haigh and Robert H. Ruby.

Thanks also for cartography assistance from Jonathan Wyss, topazmaps.com.

Picture taken during Dan Pullen–Seth Baxter litigation. Left to right, first row: Merrill Whittier, Peter Fisher, Charlie Harris, A.J. "Salvation" Smith, Dan Pullen, Frank Balch, Eph Pullen, Ely Peterson Second row: Nellie Esworthy, Jennie M. Tyler, Hattie Pullen, Emma Carpenter. Top row: David T. Smith, John Sutherland, Charles Maxfield, E.A. Esworthy, Oliver W. Smith, John Carnes, George Cooper.
Clallam County Historical Museum Collection

Note: Certain conventions, not necessarily agreed upon in the larger literary community have been arbitrarily chosen for the purposes of this book.

Native (capitalized) will be the default term for Native Americans. The word Indian will also be used when there is no risk of ambiguity and style dictates, as in Indian Treaty, or Indian Reservations. Also the Chinook word for woman/women "Klootchman" will be used for both singular and plural case.

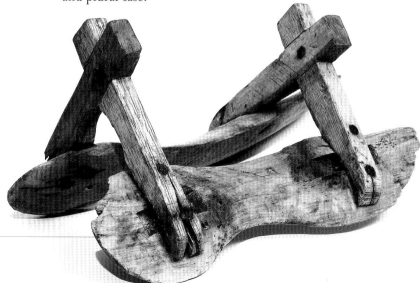

CHRONOLOGY

1775—Bodega y Quadra's Spanish galleon *Senora* loses landing party to Indians near the Hoh River.

1808—Russian ship, the *Sv. Nikolai* runs aground at LaPush, all aboard are captured and enslaved.

1832—Nisqually House established as first trading post and agricultural settlement in Puget Sound.

1843—City of Victoria founded.

1844—The Oregon Territory is created with Joseph Lane as Territorial Governor.

1846—Arguments with England over the ownership of the Oregon Territory are settled when the 49th Parallel is fixed. England retains Vancouver Island.

1848—Gold is discovered in California bringing thousands of settlers to the West.

1851—First settler arrives in Port Townsend and finds approximately 500 Indians living on the beach just above high tide.

1852—Settlement of Dungeness area begins at Whiskey Flats.

1855—Point no Point Treaty concluded; Gibbs' census shows 926 Klallams.

1855-58—Indian Wars

1856—Rufus Holmes—first permanent settler at Port Angeles (called in early days Old Dungeness, False Dungeness, or Cherbourg).

1859—James Swan's Port Townsend census shows 300 whites and 200 Klallams.

1862—Customs House moved from Port Townsend to Port Angeles.

1863—Customs House in Port Angeles destroyed when a dam created by a natural landslide breaks after heavy rain, sending a wall of water down Valley Creek. Two men die in flood.

1865—Victor Smith dies in a shipwreck off coast of northern California.

1868—Territorial Legislation forms Quillayute County.

1869—Quillayute County abolished.

1869—Dungeness massacre—last intertribal warfare involving Klallams.

1872—Daniel Pullen and Frank Balch come to Quillayute country and establish trading posts.

1875—Jamestown established.

1878—Ford Family settles Upper Prairie. (Forks Prairie)

1882—Shaker Church established in South Sound.

1887—Puget Sound Cooperative Colony moves to Port Angeles.

1889—Land boom sweeps Port Angeles waterfront. In one year population grows from 500 to 3000.

1889—Quileute Reservation is established by President Cleveland's executive order.

1889—Native village at LaPush burns.

1889—Press Expedition

1891—Port Angeles Opera House built.

1892—John Huelsdonk, "Iron Man of the Hoh," settles Upper Hoh River

1893—Panic of 1893 grips country. First National Bank of Port Angeles closes doors wiping out savings of many.

1896—First irrigation ditch brings water to Sequim Prairie

1897—Olympic Forest Reserve established by President Cleveland.

1900—Rixon and Dodwell complete Olympic Forest Reserve survey and timber cruise.

1924—Indian Citizenship Act declares Indians to be U.S. citizens.

1938—Olympic National Park formed.

1974—February 12th U.S. District Court Judge George Boldt renders his decision against the State of Washington and in favor of Indian Treaty Rights.

2005—Graving yard archeological discoveries on Port Angeles waterfront.

PREFACE

A Prelude to Settlement

In the early 1850s, Natives of what would become Washington Territory (1853) watched nervously as new-comers arrived by land and sea. These white people were not the trappers and traders of the previous two decades but were farmers and townspeople who brought families and livestock, built houses and barns, and cleared forests and plowed prairies. As the cross-state council of war convened in 1854 near present-day Tulalip, Washington, Owhi (Yakima) sounded the alarm. He argued that Native people had little time left. They must use their present numerical advantage to drive out the whites. Many of those present agreed; however, among the dissenters was Klallam Chief Chet-ze-moka who had previously been treated to a San Francisco trip hosted by far-sighted Port Townsend founders. He had seen the future and understood the futility of the proposed fight.

Chet-ze-moka spoke eloquently on the side of peace and later, while this cauldron of unrest continued to boil, forty-seven Klallam leaders including Chet-ze-moka, signed the fourteen-article Treaty of Point-No-Point. Similar treaties were signed by tribes throughout Washington territory, all negotiated by Governor Isaac Stevens and his emissaries. These agreements, often signed with little understanding and much coercion, promised peace but became a prelude to war. All too soon their implications became apparent to tribes throughout the territory. On the west side of the Cascades, Natives were dislocated, while on the east side railroad surveyors and gold seekers continued to trespass on Indian land with impunity. A pent up "tempest of hostilities" unleashed itself on the region beginning with what became known as the White River Massacre (Ruby).

On October 28, 1855, a band of Muckleshoots led by Chief Nelson and aided by two Klickitat bands attacked a settlement between present-day Kent and Auburn, Washington, killing eight and capturing a two-year-old child. The following day Chief Leschi, the South Puget Sound leader who had ordered the attacks, was approached by a peace mission consisting of Lieutenant James McAllister and Michael Connell. Both Mc Allister and Connell were killed.

Settlers got the message loud and clear. Many left the region and the rest built twenty-two stockades in Puget Sound country that were used for the next sixteen months.

Whidbey Island Blockhouse - Used during Indian Wars, 1856 - 1858.
Glenn King Collection

Although most pitched battles were to take place east of the mountains, the west side had its share of harassing raids with attendant death and destruction of property. November 26, 1855 Lieutenant Slaughter and twelve men were killed in an attack near present-day Auburn and later on January 26, 1856, a band of 800 eastside warriors made a serious effort to annihilate the Seattle population. The attempt was sabotaged by friendly local Natives with help from the *Decatur*, a U.S. warship. As fighting continued through March of 1856, a frustrated Governor Stevens ordered the arrest of a number of men of mixed marriages as well as British citizens who were accused of aiding the enemy.

Of much concern to the settlers of the Olympic Peninsula was the northern front of the war. Historically, Natives from the Canadian side of the border felt it their duty and privilege to raid Puget Sound for heads, slaves and plunder. White settlers were not seen as a threat to this tradition but an added attraction. The war simply brought additional opportunity. Port Townsend citizens complained bitterly of constant thievery and in late 1856 the steamer *Hancock* came to their aid and drove off some sixty marauding Northerners. On October 20, 1856 another flotilla of canoes and 117 raiders met their match in the person of Commander Swartout and his warship, the *Massachusetts*. Overtaken at Port Gamble and failing to grasp the gravity of their situation, the Natives defied the Commander's repeated order to return home. Twenty-seven raiders were killed and twenty-one wounded in the ensuing cannon barrage. Among those killed was a northern chief.

A blood feud had begun. The following spring North Sound settlers were sent scurrying to their block houses by the arrival of 400 painted Hiada, Tlinget and Bellabellas. To satisfy their blood feud debt with the Americans, along with the rest of their booty, the Natives left the region with the head of I.N. Ebey, customs collector on Whidbey Island.

With the death of Indian agent Andrew J. Bolon on September 23, 1856, fighting escalated east of the Cascades. Two weeks later, in what has become known as the Battle of Toppenish, Major Grandville O. Haller's Fourth Infantry[*] suffered an embarrassing defeat by a coalition of Yakimas, Sinkeuses, Wallawallas, Cayuses, Polouses, Chelans and Spokanes, losing all of their horses, cattle, and a howitzer. Motivated and emboldened by this victory, eastside Natives fought on for another two years while Native resistance in Puget Sound country was broken by their defeat at Connell's Prairie on the White River and the eventual capture of Leschi, November 13, 1856. Chief Leschi was betrayed by his nephew for fifty blankets. Many friends in the white community as well as mitigating evidence could not stop the hanging of Leschi on February 19, 1858.

For all his personal failings Klallam Chief Chet-ze-moka worked hard to maintain a neutral position for his tribe and peace on the Peninsula, often at considerable risk to his life, position and reputation. In the fall of 1857 the Chief's skill as a negotiator was to be tested again. While the rest of the Territory licked their battle wounds, discontent grew in the ranks of the Klallam. A war council was convened near what is now North Beach (Port Townsend). The ugly mood of the conference was fueled by hurt feelings and bad whiskey. Considerable sentiment was expressed for annihilating the entire Port Townsend white population. Fearing the worst, Chet-ze-moka alerted the townspeople and devised a system of signals to communicate with his white friends. Nine days running, the Chief went to what is now called Sentinel Rock and gave the danger sign. On the tenth morning Chet-ze-moka threw off his blanket giving the clear signal, thus ending the threat to peace and securing his place in Washington history.

Meanwhile on the eastside fighting continued until September 1858 when Colonel George Wright crushed the Native Confederation in the Battle of Spokane Plains. The Colonel hung Yakima Chief Qualchin and several other eastside leaders. To make the event more decisive and memorable, he also ordered the slaughter of 700 Indian ponies.

A decade that had begun with so much hope for peace and prosperity ended in so much anger, suspicion and grief. The stresses of this period and the following years of the Civil War continued to blight the Northwest well into the 1870s adding to the burden of life in the wilderness. The women who survived and in many cases thrived during this period were not ordinary women. Each one has a fascinating story. They are all "women to reckon with." Enjoy the stories of a few of these women provided on the following pages.

* Haller was later assigned the task of establishing Fort Townsend. The Major appeared still later in Port Angeles as a founding member of the Cherberg Townsite Company.

Anna Petrovna

First White Woman to Washington: The Tragedy of Anna Petrovna

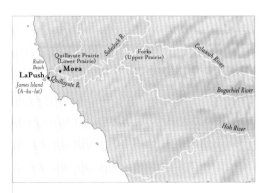

Novembor 1, 1808: After two days of a deadly dance with the rocks and reefs of the Olympic Peninsula shoreline, with three broken anchor cables and a shattered foreyard, the crippled Russian-American Company Brig, *Sv. Nikolai* rode a westerly swell into the surf and was cast ashore. Twenty-two desperate crew members including the captain's wife, Anna Petrovna, evacuated the ship to the beach north of A-ka-lat, the sheer-walled fortress of the Quileute tribe. On what is now Rialto Beach, the Russians pitched tents of sail fabric and began to salvage the vessel. They were soon approached by local Natives and the greeting was not friendly. Communications deteriorated from words to rocks, then arrows, spears, harpoons and bullets before the Natives finally withdrew. Three Quilutes were killed and all eighteen Russians not shipboard were wounded. Having worn out their welcome at La Push, the castaways broke camp the following day on November 2. They headed south toward the safety of their sister ship, the *Kodiak*, soon to be anchored in Grays Harbor. Six days later twenty-two wet, exhausted shipwreck victims stumbled into the Hoh River Valley after enduring twenty-two miles of swamps, swollen streams, the jungle of coastal forests and continual hazing by a determined contingent of very unhappy Quileutes.

At the mouth of the Hoh arrangements were made with local villagers for crossing. Nine Russians were seated in a large canoe brought from the south side.

Anna Petrovna, two Aleut women, and Filip Kotelnikov, the young apprentice, were seated in a smaller boat. At mid-river plugs were pulled from

Editor's Notes:

September 29, 1808 the *Sv. Nikolai* under the command of Navigator Nikolai Isaakovich Bulygin departed Sitka, Alaska for the coasts of Oregon Country. The voyage was conducted under a special commission from Alexander Baranov, Governor of Russian America, for the purpose of locating agricultural and trading sites between the Strait of Juan de Fuca and Northern California. The multitalented Timofei Tarakanov functioned both as bookkeeper for the voyage and personal representative of the Governor. Had the events of this adventure taken a different turn, it is likely that the first settlers on the Olympic Peninsula would have been Russian speakers. At the very least the "loss of the *Nikolai* and the marooning of its crew was no small setback for the future of Russian influence along the Pacific seaboard of North America" (K. Owens).

The Hobuckets of La Push have in their family oral history the story of this shipwreck and its aftermath. This following account, from a different cultural perspective to be sure, is based on the journal and debriefing of Timofei Tarakanov on his return to Sitka, Alaska in the summer of 1810.

THE QUILLAYUTE RIVER AND JAMES ISLAND FROM SUNSET TRAIL, MORA WN.

Opposite: "The Wreck of the Sv. Nikolai" in acrylic by Jack Datisman.

Above: Mouth of Quillayute with James Island. *Fanny Taylor photo*

Hole in the Wall - LaPush. Site of the wreck of the *Sv. Nikolai*

arrow. After repelling the attack, Tarakanov, Bulygin and the rest of the survivors escaped into the wilderness. They wandered through the forest avoiding warriors and growing hungrier by the day. By the eleventh day they had eaten the soles of their mukluks and their gun covers.

On November 12, supercargo Timofei Tarakanov wrote in his journal, "We resolved to eat our faithful dog." This was the breaking point for Bulygin who gave up his command position to Tarakanov. From the mouth of the Hoh the Russians worked their way along the river thirteen miles to where they built a fort and sustained themselves on food from neighboring fish camps. On occasion Anna was brought up stream in attempts to exchange her for rifles, terms to which her husband readily agreed but the crew vetoed. During the second week of February 1809 discipline in the group collapsed. In the midst of negotiations for her release Anna announced her satisfaction with the present situation at a Makah village and firmly refused to join her comrades. In fact, she encouraged them to join her. Five, including Tarakanov and a totally distraught Bulygin, decided thus and the rest resolved to paddle to Destruction Island which only delayed their ultimate fate.

In time the castaways were living as slaves in villages from Neah Bay to the Columbia River. According to Tarakanov, "Nikolai Isaakovich Bulygin and his wife Anna suffered the bitterest fate. At times they were together, at times separated, and they lived in continual fear they would be parted forever" (Chevigny). While Anna shared her fears with Tarakanov, he records no complaints or grumbling as she bravely faced her future. In the summer of 1809 Anna came into the hands of an especially abominable master. When she died in August, he did not permit a burial but ordered her body thrown into the forest.

So ended the tragic life of young Anna Petrovna Bulygin, wife of Chief Navigator Nikolai Isaakovich—first white woman to come to the Olympic Peninsula and indeed to the entire Pacific Northwest. On May 6, 1810, twenty months after the wreck of the *Sv. Nikolai*, the American ship *Lydia* under the command of Captain T. Brown dropped anchor in Neah Bay. On board Tarakanov was surprised to find Bolgusov who had been sold to someone on the Columbia River and subsequently purchased by Captain Brown. The Captain offered to do likewise in Neah Bay.

the hull of the larger canoe and the Native paddlers jumped overboard. Using their muskets as paddles, the Russians were able to maneuver the sinking vessel back to the north shore. The smaller canoe with Anna and her three companions continued to the south shore where an audience of two-hundred Hoh, Quileute and Quinault had gathered. As Anna's canoe landed, a confederation of warriors launched an attack back across the river. In the ensuing battle many were injured on both sides, two Native warriors were killed, and the Russian Sobachnikov was mortally wounded by an

1775—Bodega y Quadra's Spanish galleon *Senora* loses landing party to Indians near the Hoh River.

SLAVES

Until treaties were ratified in 1859, and actually for some time thereafter, slavery was a fact of life in Northwest Coast Native culture. Being taken in a night raid or while clamming or berry picking was the most terrifying future a young girl could contemplate.

In the status-conscious world of coastal society a girl's life was over; she and her descendents were stuck forever on the first rung of the social ladder. For a few fortunate ones, their important family found them, bought them back and then tried to wipe out the disgrace with a huge feast and giveaway (Underhill). A much more likely scenario would be to find oneself several days after capture being sold at the market at Oregon Falls, The Dalles on the Columbia River or the market at present-day Victoria, British Columbia.

War and raids were not the only paths to slavery. Unlike Natives to the east, Northwest coastal people had acquired a highly developed appreciation for wealth and its close relative—debt. Fines, marriage payments and other required gifting, as well as bad gambling investments and "doctor" bills, could be disastrous in a society without bankruptcy laws. Extreme measures were often taken. Cruel men sold orphaned or widowed relatives while others sold themselves to cover

unmanageable debt. In rare cases a man who sold himself could redeem himself. For all others, slavery was permanent throughout the generations even to eternity.

Slaves who were killed to be with their dead masters went to the "place of the dead" of their new tribe. However, other than an occasional ceremonial killing, slaves were not mistreated for fear they would find "power" in their suffering. Although not always the case, they often were treated as part of the family, eating and sleeping in the same house and working side by side with their owners. In some villages, lower classes lived separately and in strategically placed housing built on the first line of defense.

Slaves were their own category at the bottom of tribal hierarchy. They were spoken to in diminutive terms, and their heads were kept round as a sign of inferiority (no head flattening). Marriage to a free person was forbidden. Slaves were also limited to menial labor and restricted from those occupations requiring "power" such as hunting, whaling, carving and medicine.

Social stratification of the North Olympic Peninsula Native population has been slow to erode and though Indian slavery was officially abolished in 1859, George Pettitt wrote in a study done eighty-five years later:

There is no longer a slave class among the Quileute, but the descent of a present-day Quileute from an ancestor who was a slave in the days when there were slaves is not forgotten. No amount of personal effort or intrinsic worth has overcome that taint of heredity, even though the slave may have been a person of good blood and high ability from another tribe.

After much parlay and the eventual seizure of a Makah royal to speed negotiations, Captain Brown purchased thirteen castaways (seven of the original crew had died in captivity including Bulygin and Anna). Each person cost five blankets, thirty-five feet of woolen cloth, a file, two steel knives, one mirror, five packets of gun powder and five packets of small shot. One Russian had been sold to a distant tribe and remained with them and another was recovered by Captain George Eayres of the American ship *Mercury* on the Columbia River.

On May 10, 1810 the *Lydia* set sail from Neah Bay and June 9, Captain Brown delivered fourteen Russians to their home port of Sitka, Alaska.

1808—Russian ship, the Sv. Nikolai runs aground at LaPush, all aboard are captured and enslaved.

Above: Longhouses at LaPush. Late 1800s. *Beckstead Collection*

Opposite A.W. Smith with Native couples, 1890s, LaPush.
Beckstead Collection

A.W. Smith was "teacher, mayor, dentist and missionary."
From 1883 to 1905 he was the principal interpreter between
the Quileute and white civilization. (Pettitt)

Quālet's Gift: The Suzanne Simmons Story

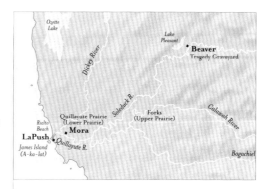

Long ago when the graves of the chiefs were canoes hung in trees on A-ka-lat, when Quileute warriors challenged neighboring tribes in battle and in bone games, when young men swam in the winter surf preparing to take on the gray whale, when the fish traps of Quileute country filled many times every winter, when the cost of a good wife was about 150 blankets and a slave could be bought for about the same amount, when Duskiya, the kelp-haired child snatcher, lurked in the forest and the feared "Doctor" Obi practiced his art, when on winter nights the murmur of conversation and story telling drifted from the smokehouses along the beach—it was in that time long ago that Quālet' was born to a sub-chief of the Quileute and his wife. Nurtured in the ways of the Quileute, Quālet' was taught how to dig and bake camas, how to gather mussels and clams and prepare them, to dry and preserve salmon and how to do her part when Joe Pullen or California Hobucket or one of the other whalers and their crews beached a monster of the deep.

Quālet' learned where in-season strawberries by the basketful could be found on the Upper Prairie (Forks Prairie). During cedar bark gathering trips into the forest she was taught and expected to sing the songs of thanksgiving to the cedar tree that accompanied the harvest of its bark. After thanking the tree for its bark, this song justified the necessity of the tree's sacrifice and explained its benefit to the Indian people. Finally the song appealed for aid in the harvest so that the tree would give up its bark in long straight strips, useful in making hats, capes, skirts, ropes, baskets, mats and numerous other household items. Quālet's

Editor's Notes:

Chris Morgenroth was an explorer, adventurer, mountain man, trail blazer, road builder and homesteader. He was also the first Ranger of District I of the Olympic National Forest and by all accounts the single person most responsible for the creation of the Olympic National Park. In the history and mythology of the Olympic Peninsula no name looms larger than that of Chris Morgenroth. The place names Morgenroth Lake (in the Seven Lakes Basin) and Morgenroth Creek (near his Bogachiel River homestead) give credit and recognition to Chris. His autobiography, *Footprints in the Olympics*, further preserves his legacy. In this comprehensive account of Chris's life and achievements, four lines of text are given to his first marriage. In a way, this is notable since Native wives (Klootchman) are seldom mentioned at all in the historical record. Their stories are found only in the closely held family oral history and lore of their descendents, in this case the Morgenroths of LaPush.

nimble fingers were trained to use the gift of the cedar. During these early years the Hoquat (Europeans) were a novelty at LaPush and Quälet' was immersed in the language, culture, myth and legend of the Quileute.

However, an east wind had begun to blow, softly at first, with the arrival of explorers, trappers and fur traders. The wind died down at times only to return with more intensity and power (Pettitt). Trader Dan Pullen arrived with a quick

gun and an iron fist. The Balch's general store was established on the north side of the river and Baxter's trading post on the south side, in LaPush. Settlers came claiming the Upper and Lower Prairies to the east. Among the first in 1878 were A. J. "Salvation" Smith, his wife, Mary, and six of his children. A short time later, after a teaching stint in Neah Bay, the Smith's oldest son, Alanson Wesley, arrived. Life changed for Quälet' when in 1883 A. W. established the first school in LaPush. A.W. Smith was a man with a mission and that mission was to civilize the local Native children even if it killed him or them. It very nearly did both at numerous times in the following twenty years.

The first order of business for Smith was the assignment of European names for everyone in the village. Quälet' was given the name Suzanne Simmons. Next was the problem of clothes. Smith made the persuasive argument that the discipline he dispensed was more tolerable for those students who were fully clothed. In the LaPush community at large Smith then took on, with varying degrees of success, head flattening, tattooing, potlatching, gambling, healing rituals by shamans, puberty rites for girls, vision quests for boys, slavery, "ceremonial excesses," use of intoxicants, and the job of imposing legal marriage and divorce on the Quileutes.

Above: A-ka-lat (James Island - Quileute Fortress)
Polhamus Collection

Left: Quileute Camp. 1900.
Polhamus Collection

1832—Nisqually House established as first trading post and agricultural settlement in Puget Sound.

In this era of cultural confusion "Susie," as she would come to be called, navigated her teenage years. There were other pressing issues facing the Quileute. The treaty of 1855-56 required the Quileute people to move to the Quinault Reservation and in Dan Pullen's mind this made the Quileute Natives, squatters on his homestead. In an effort to resolve the problem the Quileute Reservation was created Feb. 19, 1889 by executive order of President Grover Cleveland. Pullen countered the move by citing the "existing valid rights" clause in the order. So it was that the tribe returned from South Sound hop picking late in the summer of 1889 to find only a fenced field and blackened ruins where the village once stood. Housing was hastily built on available, flood prone areas near the beach. Here the Quileutes suffered through the notorious winter of `89-`90. Susie survived this period, very likely as a newlywed in Quinault country, but the world she knew as a child did not.

In the fire of 1889, the Quileutes of LaPush lost their homes and most of

Susie Morgenroth near home at LaPush.

Lela Mae Morgenroth collection.

Susie was earmarked and tatooed for identification in case of capture by enemy tribe.

Susie - middle, Marian - upper left, Lela Mae - upper right.

Marian Schumack Collection

their sacred objects, symbols, icons and artifacts. This was only the beginning of their grief. By the end of the next decade the Upper and Lower Prairie had been settled so that hunting and gathering opportunities were reduced. White fishermen were competing for salmon and whales were disappearing off the coast. A generation was growing up at LaPush without guardian spirits. Spirits now came in bottles, drink that gave visions but no power. Social institutions of the Quileutes also suffered. The old construct of arranged marriages with gift

Native woman adamantly insists on payment for picture. LaPush in 1920s.

Susie also supplemented her income with fees paid by photographers.
Glenn King Collection (Glenn)

exchanges and ceremony had been severely compromised. At the same time, the white version of marriage had not been successfully implemented by the Indian agent (A. W. Smith).

Into this spiritual/cultural vacuum came Shakerism. Susie embraced the new religion with enthusiasm. For her, as well as a large number of Quiletue, the Shaker church, with its comfortable blend of both familiar and new manifestations of power, provided an officially sanctioned path back to spiritual security. Several years before Shakerism swept LaPush, a nineteen-year-old German immigrant, Chris Morgenroth

arrived (1890) after having staked his homestead claim on the Bogachiel River. While in LaPush records show he and a friend bought 700 pounds of provisions and transported them 28 miles back to their respective homesteads by canoe. With trading posts at both LaPush and Mora, the mouth of the Quillayute River was the center of commerce for the region. It is likely that Chris visited LaPush quite frequently. His journal mentions a sealing trip in 1893 and a near disastrous canoe freighting trip from LaPush to Neah Bay in 1895. In 1896 Chris hunted fur seals in Alaska waters. While in Dutch Harbor he had a close call with gold fever when he was exposed to the sight of a poke of gold dust. The fever subsided and Chris returned to the Olympic Peninsula where he explored the upper reaches of both the North and South Forks of the Hoh River.

According to Chris's daughter/editor, Katherine Morgenroth Flaherty, Chris married Susie around 1900. Subsequent to her return from Quinault after an unhappy first marriage, Susie moved to Chris's Bogachiel River homestead and there maintained, defended, and helped prove up* on the property. She also bore Chris's four children—Nelson, Mae, Chris Jr. and Suzanne. During the ensuing years the responsibilities of maintaining the household and farm fell increasingly on Susie's shoulders as Chris spent more and more time away from home.

Concurrent with his lengthening absences, Chris's European influence over the household waned. He objected to this state of affairs and to the fact that Susie, in Quileute tradition, was quick to share family resources with Native friends and family. The Quileute protocol in this regard was as strict as it was ancient. One sought and maintained social position by gifting. Describing this period of Chris's life, Katherine Morgenroth Flaherty writes that he was "exuberant, high-spirited and restless," a "free spirit looking for direction…" It appears that by 1905 when Chris was sworn in as a U. S. Forest Ranger he had found "direction." The mountain man, adventurer, settler, explorer phase of his life was coming to a close and his homestead, kids and klootchman wife had become somewhat of an inconvenience to his meteoric rise in the agency. Chris moved out and Susie

*To fulfill government requirements necessary for the acquisition of legal title to homestead property—improvements, residency, etc.

1844—The Oregon Territory is created with Joseph Lane as Territorial Governor.

Shaker meeting LaPush 1912
This sect is not to be confused with the Shakerism of the eastern United States but is a West Coast phenomenon begun by John Slocum, a Squaxin Indian. According to Shaker church history, Slocum was an evil doer who died and came back to life a reformed man. The liturgy of the church was drawn from a mix of Protestant, Catholic and Old Indian religion (Shamanism). Woman with clasped hands on right has been identified as Susie Morgenroth.

Peterson Collection

Several years after the picture below was taken, Marian attracted the attention of a "Coasty" stationed at the Destruction Island Lighthouse. Grandmother Susie, skeptical of his intentions, gave the young man a traditional Quileute "suitor's welcome" attended by extended family. The "Coasty" was seated by the door and mercilessly questioned, admonished and exhorted in Quileute and Chinook with a little English thrown in. Uncle Chris gave an animated and embellished translation. Lela Mae and Marian hid in the kitchen. With her eyes closed and her ears covered, Marian expected the boy to bolt at any moment and visualized the long, lonely life of a spinster that would surely be hers. Marian's two-hour long nightmare was finally interrupted by Lela Mae, "Marian, Marian, you are going to be married!"

Marian Penn and Wesley Schumack were married the second day of Wesley's next shore leave as promised, using a military waiver to avoid the mandatory three day waiting period. They were happily married for 51 years and had five children together.

moved back to LaPush. In the fall of 1909 Chris attended ranger school at the University of Washington and later that year was appointed Ranger of the newly minted 600,000 acre District I of the Olympic National Forest. In 1910 Chris, with his new wife, Katherine Spease, settled in Port Angeles where District headquarters was being located.

Insult was added to injury when on her return to the reservation Susie found that she was unwelcome in LaPush and shunned for marrying a Hoquat and having his children. She was further devastated to learn through the Office of Indian Affairs that her charge of desertion and non-support had been denied since there was no record of her marriage to Chris. For years Susie lived in the most undesirable circumstances on the reservation boundary until she was finally allowed back into LaPush. Through her tribulations Susie remained loyal to the Quileute culture. Her children and grandchildren were taught the old ways by this woman of the village with scars on her arms and sorrow on her face, who wore no shoes and spoke only Quileute. The treasury of Native values, traditions, songs, stories and skills Susie carried from the 1870s into the 1950s imparts a precious legacy to now the fifth generation of her descendents. It is Suzanne Morgenroth's gift to the wider world as well.

Marian near the LaPush school house.

1846–Arguments with England over the ownership of the Oregon Territory are settled when the 49th Parallel is fixed. England retains Vancouver Island.

PAGE 23

PORTION OF PORT ANGELES WATER FRONT AND HARBOR SHOWIN PEOPLES WHARF
AND EDIZ H...
A.WISCHMEYER
...1ST 4 AVE, SEATTLE WASH.
...SON'S DRUG STORE PUBLISHERS

First Mother of Port Angeles: Caroline Smith

I f Victor Smith was Father of Port Angeles, then Caroline Smith was Mother, building homes for her family wherever life's adventures took her. In his unpublished memoir, *Victory*, Norman Smith described his mother as "golden-haired blue-eyed 'sweet-souled' Callie," whose strength and courage bolstered her graceful exterior.

Caroline's father, Nathaniel Rogers, published an abolitionist newspaper in Concord, New Hampshire. She married another abolitionist, Victor Smith (also a newsman), and set up housekeeping in Cincinnati, Ohio. According to her son, Caroline practiced her abolitionist beliefs; she transported fugitive slaves from one stop to another on their road to freedom in Canada. The election of Abraham Lincoln and its aftermath of Civil War brought upheaval to the Smith household, which now included Nellie, Warriner and Norman. Victor, a political friend of new Secretary of the Treasury Salmon P. Chase, went to Washington D.C. in the spring 1861. Put in charge of material for construction of a bridge at Harper's Ferry, Virginia, he sent for his family who came by stagecoach and train for a short stay.

Victor's appointment as special treasury agent and collector of customs for the Puget Sound district started Caroline and her children on an odyssey around the continent to Port Townsend. She already was pregnant with the couple's fourth child when the family embarked from New York in May 1861 on the steamship *Northern Light*. An ox cart with slices of logs for wheels bumped them across the Isthmus of Panama to meet the *Orizaba*, which struck a rock and limped into San Francisco. The Smiths' trip continued on the steamer *Active* to Portland, where Victor hired Indians and canoes to take his group downriver to connect with the muddy wagon road to Olympia. From here the steamer *Eliza Anderson* landed the Smith family at Port Townsend on July 30, 1861.

Victor didn't take long making enemies of most of Port Townsend. He may already have invested in land at Port Angeles in the belief that this protected harbor

From Peterson Collection

across from Victoria would make a better port of entry than Port Townsend. The citizens of Port Townsend did not agree and the fight was on. Being outgunned both literally and figuratively, the town took the battle to Callie in a campaign of terror. Callie did not terrify. Victor kept his political pull and the port of entry was moved.

As Callie's pregnancy neared its end, Victor wanted a Smith to be the first white child born in Port Angeles. In spite of stormy weather and an uncompleted new home, Callie boarded the revenue cutter *Joe Lane* November 29, 1861 for the move to Port Angeles. Nature intervened before they cleared Townsend Bay. Sailors rowed the laboring Callie ashore at the Briggs farm, where she gave birth to a daughter. Victor assuaged his disappointment by naming her Margaret Angela in honor of Port Angeles.

Although it would take several more months to complete the customs house transfer, in early 1862 Callie and the children moved to a temporary home that doubled as a surgery (physician's office) and Indian trading post at Port Angeles. The Klallam people in their village at Ennis Creek overwhelmingly outnumbered the handful of settlers who had displaced another Indian village further west on the harbor. The gentle Callie seemed instinctively to understand the Klallam way of relating through mutual gift giving and served as a peacemaker. Her hot-tempered brother-in-law Henry Smith was running the store when Old Hunter of the Klallams brought venison to trade. In a misunderstanding over weight which determined payment, both resorted to violence. Callie separated the two, took Henry's gun away and faced Old Hunter's axe unarmed,

The following article is from an unnamed Victoria newspaper as quoted in *A Pioneer's Search for an Ideal Home.*

December 16, 1868

The beautiful little American town of Port Angeles (or Angels' port) which is nestled at the foot of one of the loftiest spurs of the Cascade range of mountains, in a direction nearly opposite to our own city of Victoria, has been nearly swept away by a torrent of water which burst upon it suddenly through a gorge, or ravine, which opens into the rear of the town. The calamity occurred about six o'clock on Wednesday evening last. The first intimation which the inhabitants had of the danger was a rushing, roaring sound proceeding from the gorge, and on turning their eyes thitherward they saw a great body of water several feet in height bearing upon its surface, or sweeping before it, logs, trees and stumps, rushing down upon them. Before they could even realize their danger, the flood was upon and over the greater part of the town. The customs house, a fine two-story structure, stood exactly in the path of the vast torrent, and was overturned and swept away in a moment. Of the three occupants in the customs house at the time, Dr. Gun, the collector, who was fortunately standing near the door, was the only one who escaped. His deputy, Mr. J.W. Anderson, and Capt. Wm. B. Goodell, the inspector, who were engaged in singing church music at the time, were overwhelmed with the buildings and lost their lives. Their bodies were recovered from the ruins after the water had subsided. A person who visited the town on Saturday says that the picture of ruin and desolation presented is indescribable.

The fragments of houses and hundreds of trees and stumps lie scattered in every direction, and in some places they are piled one upon another to the height of thirty feet. The face of the town site for the breadth of at least one-hundred years by one mile long is completely changed.

The accident is supposed to have been caused by the late rains and melting snow and ice in the mountains causing avalanches into the lakes at the foothills. These lakes were then overflowed, and rushing down the gorge, carried everything before them. It is said the Indians told the whites when they were laying out their town that its site was subject to overflow, but no heed was paid to the information.

By some it is thought the customs house will be returned to Port Townsend, while others believe the damage will be repaired, and that with proper care the recurrence of a calamity of the kind may be prevented.

1848—Gold is discovered in California bringing thousands of settlers to the West.

persuading him to cool down and return later. Next morning she explained the scales to him. Norman recalled:

Until Old Hunter died in 1868, the first hind quarter of every elk or deer he killed was always brought to mother as a present, and never would he take pay for it.

However, he would always accept a present from mother who took care that, in amount, it was always in the full value of the venison he brought.

By late 1862 the family moved into a permanent home built as an ell off the Customs House at the foot of Valley Street. The family's furniture and Callie's grand piano had been shipped around Cape Horn. Although she allowed her children the freedom of water and woods, Callie made certain they had the benefits of book learning and culture. She taught them to sing, and she and their father read aloud from the family library. Victor shuttled between Puget Sound, San Francisco and Washington, D.C., defending his position and persuading President Lincoln to set aside a military reservation on Port Angeles Harbor. During one of his absences in December 1863, a dam created by a natural landslide broke after heavy rains, sending a wall of water down Valley Creek. Two men died when the Customs House was swept away but Callie managed to save her children and her housekeeper. In spite of the flood Callie later told her son that 1863 and 1864 had been her happiest days.

With Chase's resignation jeopardizing his own position by late 1864, Smith made another trip to Washington, D.C. Once more, Callie and her three older children traveled by way of Panama to New York, where they replaced furnishings lost in the flood. In late May 1865, Victor was assigned to transport millions in federal dollars and bonds to San Francisco. He and his family took passage on the *Golden Rule*, whose captain may have deliberately run it aground on Roncador Reef in a plot to steal the federal treasure. The passengers subsisted on birds' eggs for several days until rescue came. Caroline and her children picked up their trip to San Francisco, where they purchased some furnishings and a cabinet organ to replace what had had been lost with the *Golden Rule* and continued to Port Angeles. Their last sight of Victor was on Roncador Reef where he remained to guard the wreck until the Coast Guard came. The federal treasure was not recovered. Victor was lost while homeward bound aboard the *Brother Jonathan*, which sank in a storm off Northern California July 30, 1865.

The pregnant Caroline was left to care for her children. On November 22, 1865, Victor Rogers Smith was born. One night later a fire destroyed their home. In poor health and unwilling to leave her children to unsympathetic in laws, Caroline married neighbor Samuel Atkinson in 1869. Caroline's family persuaded them to homestead near her brother in Iowa. She persevered to raise her family under difficult circumstances, although her marriage ended in divorce.

Worn out with caring for her mother through her last illness, Caroline returned to Port Angeles in August 1890 to live with Norman and May Smith. By now, Norman was mayor of Port Angeles which had grown to about 4,000 people and Caroline was honored as its matriarch until her death in January 1891.

Judge Marcellus Aurelius Brutus Huntoon

The first Justice of the Peace of the Port Angeles precinct of Clallam County was one-eyed, crooked-nosed Judge Marcellus Aurelius Brutus Huntoon. Judge Huntoon had a habit of convening Court just about anywhere he pleased. One settler who complained when his cabin was commandeered was cited for contempt and fined $500. When the exasperated settler complained further, Judge Huntoon explained that "Wherever I take off my hat, court is in session."

Fortunately the Judge most frequently hung his hat at home on the Elwha River or in James Dalgardno's saloon on the waterfront in Port Angeles. It was most likely at the saloon that the Klallam, Wa Hothulp, was tried for the theft of $7000 in gold coins belonging to Caroline and Victor Smith. It seems that when the flash flood on Valley Creek swept away Conklin House, John Everett's meat market and part of the customs house, it also carried out to sea a chest full of coins belonging to the Smiths.

Witnesses claimed that Wa Hothulp carried the chest to his house. Wa Hothulp was found guilty and sentenced by Judge Huntoon but the coins were never found. The verdict in this case remains in dispute. According to some, the chest full of coins lies buried in the mud at the bottom of the Port Angeles Harbor.

1851—First settler arrives in Port Townsend and finds approximately 500 Indians living on the beach just above high tide.

PAGE 27

（略）

Preacher's Daughter and Alaskan Icon: The Unsinkable Harriet Pullen

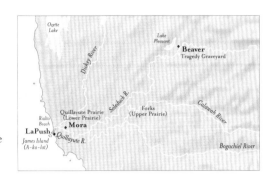

I. Harriet and the Scoundrel of Skagway

Through Skagway, Alaska's boomtown, the human financial wreckage of the '93 depression pushed, shoved and elbowed their way toward the Klondike in one glorious, desperate gamble with fate. They suffered the symptoms of a highly contagious disease that racked the body and ravaged the mind, spirit and soul—gold fever.

Gold fever infected the righteous and vile alike. The undisputed vilest of the vile came to Skagway in 1897 from Denver, Colorado in the person of Jefferson Randolph Smith. In stark contrast to the vermin that he was, Smith, known to most as "Soapy," appeared on the street in "a carefully brushed black suit, signature black sombrero and highly polished boots" (Haigh). A mixture of the venal and the respectable, the malevolent and the merciful, Soapy's ministerial face, framed by dark hair and a trimmed beard, masked his inner decay.

Soon after his arrival in Skagway, bogus business fronts, bunko schemes and a thriving extortion/protection industry infected the heart of the town. Sensitive to his public persona, he gave generously to the poor widow and the church alike but just as quickly directed his henchmen to reclaim the contributions. His benevolence extended especially to the single females of Skagway who were in need of special protection. So it was that Soapy Smith in his usual charitable spirit approached a certain pie maker with what he was sure would be a sweet deal. His miscalculation had painful consequences. The frying pan that ricocheted off his head sent Soapy's black sombrero flying.

Word spread swiftly about the notorious outlaw's encounter with a hot-headed vixen. Soapy's reputation was infamous but who was this five foot, nine inch full-figured fire-brand? Most knew her as Harriet Pullen. She identified herself as a widow who had followed the first surge of fortune seekers and "with only seven dollars in her pocket" and no means of support, had secured a job cooking for Captain William Moore, a well-respected Skagway citizen and man of means. To supplement her income, she baked apple pies using surplus dried

ONE PROSPECTOR: *I have stumbled upon a few tough corners of the globe during my wanderings beyond the outpost of civilization, but think the most outrageously lawless quarter I ever struck was Skagway. It seemed as if the scum of the earth had hastened there to fleece, and rob or to murder. There was no law whatsoever; might was right, the dead shot only was immune to danger (Haigh).*

Sun porch - Pullen House. Skagway, Alaska

Clallam County Museum Collection

apples and sold them as fast as they came out of the oven. As the pie business thrived she made plans to diversify.

Opportunities with the best potential for return often had high risk associated with them. Harriet chose a business with high-end potential and a deadly reputation. In 1898, less than a year after she arrived in Alaska, Harriet arranged to have the trail horses she still owned in Washington State shipped to Skagway. On their arrival she jumped them off the vessel's cargo deck and led them to shore using a rowboat. Within days she was geared up and freighting over the notorious White Pass Trail, a.k.a. the Dead Horse Trail named for the 3,000 pack animals that had died there in the previous season.

By the end of 1899 a railroad replaced the horses and Harriet was forced to look elsewhere to make a living. Further complicating matters, three of her four children were now living with her in cramped quarters and she needed more room. In addition, her estranged husband, Dan Pullen, had also made his way up the coast to Skagway.

With profits saved from freighting, she purchased

Captain William Moore's home and converted it into a grand hotel. Presidents, Governors and other notable public figures basked in the hotel's luxurious ambiance and delighted in Harriet's high-spirited hospitality. Her guests enjoyed hot baths and soft beds in their rooms. Harriet's meals, prepared with vegetables, freshly picked from her gardens and fresh milk and cream from her dairy, were unsurpassed. The hotel's lively entertainment often featured Harriet's dramatic presentations.

Harriet worked from a breathtaking abundance of raw material which she carefully mined and milled. Gold rush Skagway sported sixty-one saloons and an equal number of gambling establishments. Tents, shacks, and other buildings of fragile architecture housed 15,000 inhabitants. Music and dance halls were numerous and varied in elegance from the classy "Theatre Royale" to the "Bonanza," a dive where packer Joe Brooks posted a $4,700 tab in one expensive night. Women entertainers ran the gamut from dance hall queens "Montana Filly," Ethel the Moose," and "Diamond Lil Davenport" to variety theater singers, Anna (the Nightingale of the North), Minnie LaTour and Nellie LaMarr. During

1852—Settlement of Dungeness area begins at Whiskey Flats.

Dan Pullen House, 1892

Ely Peterson, a juror in the Pullen trial, sends news of the trial's progress in a letter to his wife, Winnie.

Port Angeles   June 12, 1895

Dear Winnie,

As I do not see any prospects of me coming home for a week or two, I will scribble you a few lines. I have a bad cold and I am getting tired of loafing around this place. There have been but two wit-nesses on the Pullen's side….Mrs. Pullen [has been] on the stand three days and has made lots of false statements swearing to one thing at one time and later on, dispute it. She swore that the house at the beach cost them $1200. Then they showed her testimony that she swore to in the trial at LaPush when she swore that the house cost them $5000. It looks dark for Dan. At present some think Mrs. P is the best witness Baxter has had. …I do not know when I will come home so you can run the farm as best you can.

With love to all. Your affectionate hubby,

Ely Peterson

P.S. Mrs. P told the lawyer he had asked so many questions that they were buzzing around in her head like a wheel.

Soapy' Smith's "year of glory" the line up of notables on the street included Reverend Charles Bowers—a child of the devil posing as a man of the cloth, Big Ed Burns—a heavy, Canada Bill—a cardsharp specializing in three-card-monte, Claude Alexander Conlin—the seventeen-year-old manager of Soapy's prostitution enterprises, Fatty Green—a.k.a. "Shoot your Eyes out Green" who was in charge of Soapy's complaint department, King of Terrors—his name says it all, John Light—gunfighter, Wilson Mizner—extortionist, bootlegger and murderer, "Moon-Faced Kid," "Ice Box Murphy," "Sheeney Kid," and George Wilder—investment authority and financial advisor. By some estimates there were two-hundred of Soapy's "friends" in addition to a number of brave independents.

Harriet knew all their stories and her dramatic renditions were popular with tourists at dockside as well as the parlor of Pullen House. Harriet's "Soapy Smith's Final Hour"* could only be described as a "stunner" (Clifford). All eyes were wide, mouths agape and breath stilled as Harriet, dressed in 90s costume, relived those moments and reveled in her memories. Props for her production were authentic "Soapy" artifacts that had come into her possession after his death. One of Soapy's belongings of particular interest was the painting of a nude that Harriet kept conspicuously displayed above the kitchen stove at Pullen House. Whenever Harriet's taste in décor was questioned Harriet's stern answer was always the same, "I had to put her there to keep her warm." The relationship between Soapy and Harriet has been clouded by time and voluminous Skagway myth and legend. It is unclear now whether Harriet loved Soapy or simply the

Preceding pages: Pullen family at Pullen house, with James Island in the background.
Clallam County Museum Collection

Harriet Pullen with friend Tillie Atwood. Late 1870s.
Clallam County Museum Collection

1854—Suffrage for women was defeated by the Territorial Legislature by one vote.

A.W. Smith with his students at LaPush. 1905.   *Clallam County Museum Collection*

The following article is from a January 18, 1907, issue of the Olympic Times, an early Port Angeles newspaper.

Gertrude—A Wreck

Piled Up On Slip Point Reef at Clallam Bay Last Friday Night Passengers and Crew Rescued with Difficulty from Perilous Position by Tugs *Lorne* and *Wyadda-* Experiences of Mrs. Pullen, One of the Pioneers of the West End.

The *Alice Gertrude* left East Clallam at 7:45 o'clock Friday evening on her regular trip to Neah Bay, in the teeth of a howling gale and a snow storm so thick that her master could not see a ship's length ahead. After bucking the gale for an hour or more, a steam-pipe broke in the engine room and under the conditions Captain Kalstrom decided to put back into Clallam Bay for shelter. In attempting the entrance to the harbor, with the light (Slip Point Light House) invisible by reason of the snow, and the fog horn barely audible if at all, Captain Kalstrom mistook his bearings and the Gertrude struck head-on on the rocks. Finding it impossible to back off the reef, Captain Kalstrom at once set about preparations to make sure of the safety of his passengers and crew. A terrible sea was running, making it impossible to launch the ship's [life] boats, particularly as she had listed badly and everything was frozen stiff. Rockets were burned and the predicament of the vessel made apparent to the people of the Bay, who at once began such work as practicable for the rescue of the imperiled persons aboard. The tugs *Lorne* and *Wyadda*, which were at Neah Bay, were summoned by wire, both reaching the scene before daylight but being unable to render any immediate assistance by reason of the heavy

drama he brought to her life. It is however, instructive to note that it was Harriet who tended Soapy's grave for a half century.

II. Harriet's Mansion by the Sea

Most history books acknowledge Harriet Pullen's role in civilizing the North. Few historians, however, have given much thought or pen to the 38 years she spent in the "lower forty-eight." Harriet Matilde Smith was born to A.J. and Mary Smith on August 13, 1860 in Mt. Hope, Grant County, Wisconsin. Soon after A. J. "Salvation" returned home from his Civil War duties as secretary to General Beadle, he made plans to move his family west.

In 1869 "Salvation" arrived in Yankton, Dakota Territory. Yankton boasted spectacular lakes, magnificent rivers and verdant stands of deciduous trees. In later years this Dakota Territory capitol provided respite for gold seekers en route to the Black Hills. Preferring the countryside to town or city, A. J. settled his family on a remote prairie homestead. Here living in a home of South Dakota sod, nine-year-old Harriet learned the harsh realities of frontier life and proved her metal. On one occasion when fire swept the prairie threatening the livestock, she drove all the farm animals into the river to save them. Five years later at fourteen during a blizzard and with A. J. again absent, Harriet served as midwife for her mother. Three of Harriet's seven siblings were born on the Dakota prairie.

For eight years the Smith family endured hostile weather, cruel isolation, and intermittent sickness. In the end, it was the destructive work of grasshopper plagues that drove the family further west. In the early spring of 1877, the same

1855—Point no Point Treaty concluded; Gibbs' census shows 926 Klallams.

PAGE 35

Mrs. Pullen and Pullen House Bus in Ea

PULLEN HOUSE.

LEN HOUSE

Printed by Dedmans
Photo Shop.

Dedman
123

Days

seas. In the meantime, a line was shot ashore and a breeches-buoy was rigged for use as a last resort in reaching shore. Being satisfied that all hands were safer aboard than in trying to reach shore before daylight, Captain Kalstrom reassured all and kept them as comfortable as possible during the night.

After daylight on Saturday the tugs which had been standing by began trying to take off the passengers and crew. The seas, having subsided somewhat, boats were launched from the tugs, and a life raft was swung over the side of the *Gertrude* on which the people aboard were pulled thru the water several at a time to the small boats, taken aboard the tugs and landed at the wharf three-quarters of a mile away.

The hero of the rescue work, from all accounts, was Captain Butler, of the big British tug *Lorne*, who manned one of his whale boats himself and directed the work of taking the people off the raft and from the water.

Among the passengers, and the only white woman who underwent the hardships of the wreck, was Mrs. Dan Pullen, the former well-known pioneer resident of Lapush, but now of Skagway, Alaska. Mrs. Pullen, although

Steamer Alice Gertrude on rocks at Clallam Bay

year Jack McCall was convicted and hung in Yankton for gunning down the legendary Wild Bill Hickok, Harriet, her parents and seven siblings boarded a train headed for the Pacific Northwest. The family completed their journey shipboard and arrived in Neah Bay April 7, 1877. Unfortunately, their arrival coincided with an outbreak of typhoid fever in the village. Little Lizzie Smith, only nine-years-old fell ill and died. Broken, but not defeated, the family retreated to Olympia, regrouped and returned six months later to Neah Bay and from there continued on to LaPush.

Dan Pullen, the tall, bearded trader/promoter at LaPush, was always helpful to newcomers, but took a special interest in this family with the seventeen-year-old statuesque red-head who exuded poise and self-confidence. Dan aided the Smiths in their choice of prime real estate on the Big Prairie (Quillayute Prairie).

Reputed to be the wealthiest settler around, Dan was a businessman who specialized in land deals. He bought 240 acres at LaPush and then purchased 640 more from family and friends. Dan also owned 320 acres on Little Prairie and another 320 acres in partnership with his brother, Mart. James Island was also on his list of prized real estate. Life had never been easy for Dan but as a young man he learned to work hard and manage his finances wisely. Born in Maine in 1842, his father died in 1849 leaving a widow with eight children, several of whom became deaf by the same fever. Tired of watching his mother struggle and feeling powerless to help, Dan ran away in 1856. Five years later, in 1861, he came west via the Isthmus of Panama, eventually ending up at a logging camp on Puget Sound. By age 28 he had made enough money to set up a trading post at LaPush. He also had earned an impressive reputation as a fierce fist fighter.

Harriet owned her own well-deserved reputation as a fighter, one that she upgraded as necessary. Not long after her marriage at age 21 to Dan Pullen, Harriet's brother, Alanson Wesley, teacher at the LaPush Indian School, raised the ire of parents over a discipline problem. The situation escalated to an issue of tribal respect and dignity. A mob of angry LaPush Natives led by "Doctor" Lester tried, convicted and was about to execute A.W. when the proceedings were interrupted by the thundering voice of Harriet speaking in Chinook Jargon. Harriet stood on the balcony of the Pullen Trading Post looking down the barrel of a rifle trained on the "Doctor." A shotgun and second rifle leaned against the railing. Harriet had established herself as a sharpshooter and no one in the mob showed the least interest in testing her skill. The crowd dispersed and later five ringleaders were sent to prison.

A year after their February 1881 marriage, the Pullens had their first child, Mildred who was educated at Western Washington Normal School and graduated from St. Mark's Hospital in New York with a nursing degree. Sons Dan (1885) and Royal (1887) both played football for the University of Washington and were decorated heroes of WWI. A third son, Chester (1889) drowned off the coast near Ketchikan on his way to his second year at the University of Washington.

Harriet's young children did not attend the La Push tribal school taught by

1856—Rufus Holmes—first permanent settler at Port Angeles (called in early days Old Dungeness, False Dungeness, or Cherbourg).

Harriet's husband and sons, Daniel Pullen with Dan, Chester and Royal. Seattle, 1906.

one of the most fearless of the passengers, underwent the most terrible experience of all, and owes her life to her own bravery and presence of mind, as much as to the work of the gallant rescuers. After she had clambered onto the life raft, when her turn came to go ashore, an unusually heavy sea raised the raft above the side of the steamer and in settling it caught on the guard-rail and was turned completely over, with Mrs. Pullen underneath in the water. Mrs. Pullen relates that she had presence of mind enough to reach up and grasp one of the slats of the raft, to which she clung for her life, and realizing her position under the raft she worked her way to the edge of it, getting her hand out and holding on till she was rescued from the water by Captain Butler's boat. Mrs. Pullen was quickly taken aboard the *Lorne* and transferred to the dock, where she was taken in charge by friends.

A portion of the mail, the freight aboard and most of the personal belongings of the passengers and crew were lost. Upon the arrival of the *Rosalie* at East Clallam Saturday afternoon the survivors were all taken aboard and brought here (Port Angeles) where they arrived at 10 p.m.

Mrs. Pullen has resided at Skagway for the past eight years where she runs one of the prominent hotels of the northern town. She had been on a visit of a week to her mother, Mrs. M. J. Smith, still residing at Quillayute. She had come out that day and took the *Gertrude* on its outward trip thinking to get a night's rest. Mrs. Pullen has two sons in the Seattle High School, one a member of the famous football team, while her oldest son is at West Point, where he also is a famous athlete.

The latest reports from the scene of the wreck are to the effect that the *Gertrude* had already practically gone to pieces. The heavy swells that for several days followed the storm soon broke her up.

her brother; instead, they were educated by a hand-picked governess. Child care and domestic chores were provided by a Quileute Indian named Sam, whom Harriet personally trained. For the first few years of their marriage, the Pullens lived a life of luxury enjoying every conceivable amenity. Their seaside mansion caught the eye of every passerby; few could have imagined that the following decade would be fraught with litigation and feuds over land and resources. A year before his marriage to Harriet, Dan sold land to the Baxter brothers who owned Washington Fur Company. Afterward he worked for them as an agent and fur buyer. The land was in the heart of the tribal village but at the time Dan acquired it, a government plan was in place to remove the Indians to a reservation near Grays Harbor. According to historian Ruby Hult in her book, *The Untamed Olympics*, after Dan got married, "bad blood developed between the

1859–James Swan's Port Townsend census shows 300 whites and 200 Klallams.

PAGE 39

Dan Pullen's House in LaPush

Pullens and the Baxters." Apparently the Baxters disliked Harriet because "she put on airs." The company accused Harriet of stealing from the store, discharged Dan and sued the Pullens for $18,000. Many of the Quillayute settlers testified for the Pullens in what proved to be the longest trial in Clallam County to that time. According to a Seattle newspaper correspondent, Harriet Pullen answered 4,000 questions during the litigation. The Baxters ultimately lost.

Hult explains in her account that following the trial the Baxter brothers left LaPush and Dan continued to operate his own fur business. Unfortunately, this trial was just a precursor of what was to come. In 1889 the Government had given the tribe a mile-square reservation at the mouth of the Quillayute River in an agreement that gave prior rights to earlier claimants. Pullen had filed a pre-emption claim in 1882 and a timber land entry in 1883 and he believed he was eligible for this exemption and prior claim. In addition, he had built what came to be called the "Pullen Mansion," a huge, two-story home with decks and bay windows and spectacular views of the dazzling Pacific seashore. The government ordered that his claim be cancelled.

Coincidentally, that same year (1889) while the Quileutes were away picking hops, their village was burned to the ground.

Dan was the prime suspect. Some said, however, that the incident was instigated by the Baxter brothers who meant to frame the Pullens. In fact, the Baxters later encouraged the Indian Agency to bring suit against the Pullens and reclaim the land for the Indians. Ultimately, Dan and Harriet won in circuit court, the circuit court of appeals and also at a land office hearing. The financial cost was devastating, however, and the Pullens were forced to mortgage all of their holdings. They retaliated by bringing suit against the Baxters but Baxter deeded everything he owned to his wife and declared bankruptcy. Subsequently the Indian Agency who unlike Dan and Harriet had deep pockets, appealed again. The Pullens failed to respond and the government won by default. By 1897, the Pullen's wealth had dissipated, and Harriet was growing increasingly dissatisfied and frustrated. The loss of income and prestige became impossible for Harriet to tolerate and she was ready to move on.

In the fall of 1897 Harriet joined Minerva Troy from Port Angeles on the Steamship *Rosalie* sailing for Skagway where in a new life she would become a cultural icon and her legacy a prized possession of the entire state of Alaska.

* Soapy Smith died on Juneau Wharf in 1898 in a shoot-out with Frank Reid

1862—Customs House moved from Port Townsend to Port Angeles.

For historians who as a profession abhor coincidence, revelations connecting Quillayute Country with the Far North generate a multitude of questions. Barring the appearance of another psychic with the talents of Claude Alexander Conlin, they will in all likelihood remain unanswered.

"The Man who Knows"

One mile north of the Senior Center at LaPush (the site of Dan and Harriet Pullen's mansion), on the bluff above Rialto Beach are terraces, walkways and foundation stones of an incredible complex. Here, nearly one-hundred years ago, the beach, Pacific Ocean, James Island and the Quillayute Needles formed an exquisite backdrop for what came to be known as "The Castle," summer home of The Great Alexander. Alexander "The Man who Knows" was a Vaudeville performer of considerable fame and reputation whose alcohol-fueled parties during prohibition were legendary for their "excesses." An endless parade of wives, groupies, and Hollywood friends commanded the ongoing interest of neighbors who were kept up to date by vigilant operators at the Forks telephone switchboard. Because of Alexander's relaxed attitude toward marriage (he married twelve times) local husbands and fathers were always a little on edge when "The One Who Knows" was in town. At least one spouse enforced his more restrictive view of the institution of marriage with a firearm.

Suspicion was not limited to the domestic front. Armed grounds keepers and activity at odd hours near the mouth of the Quillayute River caused imaginations to explore various unsavory possibilities. Stories processed in the local rumor mill expanded to opium, whiskey and human smuggling. An alleged co-conspirator on the Quillayute River was friend and fellow stampeder, J.E.L. James. James, whose four taverns in Seattle were a casualty of prohibition, bought property from K.O. Erickson in 1916 and established a hotel in Mora. Alexander was a very satisfied early customer at the hotel and, like James, was not one to ignore opportunity. So along with the bogus investment advice Alexander dispensed to his audiences while on the road, Alexander also invited the bereaved to contact their dearly departed by meeting with him in the luxury of the Mora Hotel. "Alexander had learned early in his career that real money could be made playing the role of oracle and fleecing dreamers" (Beckmann).

For "The Man Who Knows" the future was no mystery; however, only recently has his own past been revealed. In 1898 at age seventeen, Claude Alexander joined the throngs headed for Alaska. Choosing the White Pass route to the gold fields, Claude disembarked in Skagway and was promptly relieved of all his worldly goods playing a "three shell game" run by Soapy Smith's men. Soapy had mercy on the young, penniless kid, saw his potential and made him a lieutenant—in charge of prostitution management. Years later The Great Alexander wrote, "Alaska absorbed all my gullibility."

From Skagway Claude moved to the Yukon where he continued his education in the saloons of Dawson City under the tutelage of Pericles "Alexander" Pantages and Kathleen Eloisa Rockwell, also known as "Klondike Kate." After a card table shooting in 1902 Claude left the North just ahead of a lynch mob. Back in the states he married for the first time and joined a circus where he and his young bride performed an escape act. Next came a profitable run as Dr. Astro of Dr. Astro's Psychic Parlor in San Francisco which was cut short by a "Mexican vacation" that ended with Claude being extradited back to San Francisco.

In the teens Claude reconnected with Alexander Pantages who by now had become the wealthiest theater chain owner in America. (Pantages' girlfriend, Klondike Kate, who left the North with $150,000, had long since been discarded and relieved of her riches.) Claude played the Vaudeville venues of his Klondike friend, took a page from Pantages "book on women" and was soon on his way to prosperity. Claude became "The Great Alexander" who played to packed audiences and earned up to $18,000 a week from ticket sales alone. However, Alexander had earned an advanced degree in psychology and the human condition from the school of hard knocks in the Northland and he was not one to waste education. Alexander was always alert for the easy mark and the gullible sucker. Biographer Darryl Beckmann described him as "talented, charming and innovative." Beckmann also called Alexander "manipulative, ruthless, purposefully wicked and relentlessly self-serving." A womanizer with few peers, Alexander "invariably improved his financial status with each of his twelve marriages" (Beckmann).

For the fifteen years Alexander frequented Rialto, the people of Quillayute country had their suspicions, but not in their wildest imaginings could they understand the perverse evil that was in their midst. Murder, extortion, fraud, blackmail, booze and drugs—Alexander was Soapy Smith with a weakness for the ladies and a good lawyer.

1863—Customs House in Port Angeles destroyed when a dam created by a natural landslide breaks after heavy rain, sending a wall of water down Valley Creek. Two men die in flood.

Thoroughly Modern Minerva:
Minerva Troy

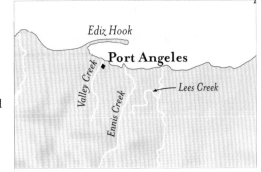

The story of Minerva Lewis Troy is one of a self-reliant, artistic, adventurous woman. The twists and turns of her life take Minerva from stage and studio in Port Angeles to the hell-hole of 1897 Skagway, Alaska where life was cheap and mafia boss Soapy Smith ruled with his gang of thugs. A broken marriage and two children later, Minerva turned up at age 44 as a Red Cross hospital volunteer in war-torn France.

Back in Port Angeles after World War I Minerva became a force to be reckoned with in the politics and culture of the region. The varied events of Minerva's life and the breadth of her interests and accomplishments frustrate description and analysis. Was she driven by ambition, narcissism, creative impulse, her spirit of adventure or was it altruism? We can only speculate as to her "motivation." In the following piece done for the 1989 State Centennial Celebration, local historian Dona Cloud tells Minerva's story. It was published in its original form in Strait History, the Historical Quarterly of the Clallam County Historical Society. Additions to the text were made by the editors to reflect recent archival discoveries.

Minerva Lewis was born in 1873 to Dr. Freeborn Stanton Lewis and his wife, Edna Thompson Lewis, who gave her all of the cultural advantages of a middle class, mid-west upbringing. It was considered unsuitable for girls to be trained for a career, but the education of young ladies was not considered complete without music and painting. Minerva showed talent in both fields. In an interview with Charlotte Widrig for the *Seattle Times*, she recalled:

> I was born with a love for painting. As a child I persisted in covering the margins
> of father's medical books with pictures. When I was 10 years old, living in
> Omaha (Nebraska), my parents arranged for my first art lessons.

Dr. Lewis came to Port Angeles in 1887 as a physician with the Puget Sound Co-operative Colony. Not certain that he wanted to continue his marriage, he arranged for his wife and daughter to live with his parents in Vassar, Michigan. However, after three years he sent for his wife and Minerva who was then 17 years old.

A lifelong friend, the late Mae Davis, describes the world of Minerva and her mother as having been "long kid gloves, slippers and dance programs. They came to a settlement of Indians, settlers, clams, fish, gardens and cows." Minerva set the social, artistic and political pattern for Port Angeles and continued throughout her life to contribute to the cultural education of its citizens.

Puget Sound Co-operative Colony people contributed their talents to a variety of entertainments and in 1891 built an Opera House that became the

Following pages: Dr. Lewis, his daughter, Minerva Troy and her daughters. Port Angeles.
Clallam County Museum Collection

In her studio at 203 East Front Street in port Angeles, Minerva Troy taught music and oil, watercolor and china painting.

Clallam County Museum Collection

center of community musical and dramatic productions. Minerva, who played organ and piano and sang in a lovely contralto voice, fit right in.

When money was needed to have a promotional painting done for the World's Columbian Exposition at Chicago in 1893, she joined her fellow citizens in presenting a light opera, *The Chimes of Normandy*. With Minerva in the lead as Germaine, the production played to a full house and earned $200 to pay the visiting German artist, Count Gustav Kallang. Minerva added to her own art education with lessons from Kallang.

In the town's first church wedding in December 1892, Minerva married John Troy at the Congregational Church, First and Vine streets. The bridegroom, a native of Clallam County, was a newspaperman who had just been elected county auditor. Minerva assisted him in both enterprises.

The Troys were young and socially active. The *Tribune Times* of February 9, 1893, gives us a window on their world:

A party of ten chaperoned by Mr. and Mrs. John W. Troy, formed a delightful sleighing party on Monday night, and although the snow was too deep for rapid locomotion, the novelty of such a ride in Port Angeles made the trip a pleasant one. After a few hours' ride the entire party went to the home of Mr. and Mrs. Troy, where they spent the remainder of the evening in a game of whist.

In 1897, John Troy joined the Klondike gold rush, but as a newspaperman at Skagway rather than as a miner. Minerva, who had stayed behind in Port Angeles, heard that John was lonesome for her. She sold all their belongings and headed for Alaska in the company of another indomitable Clallam County pioneer, Harriet Pullen, aboard the steamer *Rosalie*.

The Troy home in Alaska was a cabin on the trail to the gold fields. As organist for the boom town's Episcopal Church, Minerva played for funerals of famous gamblers, robbers, and lawmen. She sang in concerts, acted in plays and continued to paint.

1865—Victor Smith dies in a shipwreck off coast of northern California.

In the fall of 1897, John Troy returned to Seattle and Minerva stayed with Harriet Pullen who lived in a small cookhouse. Harriet slept in a cot that hung from the ceiling, while Minerva slept on a table under bearskins. She had to rise at 4 a.m. so Harriet could cook and serve breakfast to a construction crew.

In the spring, John returned to Skagway and the Troys' first daughter, Helen, was born in 1899. The following year John's serious illness required a trip to Port Angeles where Dr. Lewis treated him and he recovered. The Troy's second daughter, Dorothy, was born at Port Angeles in 1901. Upon the family's return to Skagway, both children became ill and Minerva brought them back to Port Angeles, while John stayed in Skagway.

Although Minerva returned to Alaska once more in 1903, she was not divorced from John until 1911. By 1901 she was essentially a single parent with two daughters to support. They lived with her father (alone since his divorce from Edna) in the family home at First and Oak in Port Angeles.

Art, along with teaching, writing and nursing, was one of the few respectable occupations open to women. Minerva opened a studio at 203 East Front Street in Port Angeles, where she taught music and art.

Minerva worked in watercolors and oils, painting landscapes, still lifes and portraits. Many of her paintings were copies of well-known romantic and decorative art works. She was little influenced by new art movements in the world at large. Cubism, Fauvism and Impressionism would not have impressed Minerva or fellow Port Angeles citizens as "real art." She apparently was not familiar with Emily Carr, who worked across the water in Victoria, or with another contemporary, Georgia O'Keefe.

By the turn of the century four-color printing processes had made possible the use of colorful, imaginative art work to accompany magazine stories and women were doing a lot of the illustration work. Minerva used such magazine illustrations and art prints as studies for class work.

China painting was a woman's craft and fad of the time. Minerva learned the craft from Mrs. H.B. Wilson of Seattle and in turn taught many Port Angeles women. She had a kiln to fire the china. Her own hand-painted china was in great demand. Nearly every local household had pieces of her work and she filled orders from shops around Puget Sound. Many of Minerva's china pieces still are cherished by their owners.

By 1917, Minerva's daughters had returned to Alaska, her father had died, and the U.S. had entered World War I. At the age of 44, she joined the Red Cross, took nurse's training at Port Angeles General Hospital and more specialized training in Seattle. She worked in an office to pay her expenses and lived with a former Port Angeles resident, Mrs. M.J. Carrigan.

In the summer of 1917, Minerva embarked for Paris, France, where she worked in a base hospital until troops were evacuated. She then spent eight months working for the Red Cross in the auditing department. Her return trip to the United States included visits to Italy and Spain. By Armistice Day 1919, she was back in Port Angeles.

Once again living in the family home, she supported herself as a nurse and as Red Cross executive secretary on a salary of $10 per month. She traveled throughout Clallam County in her own car doing what is now considered welfare work.

How much painting and teaching she did during the next ten years is uncertain, but Minerva kept busy with politics, now opened to women through passage of the 19th amendment.

In 1922, Minerva was persuaded to run for the U.S. House of Representatives; she was the first Washington women to try for this office. Her World War I experience dictated her campaign platform, which called for a bonus for ex-servicemen. Port Angeles newsman Jack Hensen quoted Minerva as saying, "I wasn't elected but I did get a lot of votes."

Minerva headed the Democratic Party in Port Angeles and served as state Democratic committeewoman several times. She was assignment clerk of the House of Representatives during five legislative sessions in Olympia.

Her work on local campaigns for Franklin Roosevelt and her own outstanding capabilities led to government positions. Minerva worked with the State Re-employment Service, opened the first Social Security office in the county and was an executive in the Works Progress Administration.

Under the National Recovery Act, from 1933 to 1936, Minerva was paid to teach art in her new home at 118 West Second Street.

Although described by many as a gentle person, Minerva was not afraid to fight, and fight she did when the federal government in 1930 wanted to take her family home for a post office site. Since ownership of the property was in

1869—Quillayute County abolished.

question, stemming from the opening of the Federal Townsite Reserve in the 1890s when squatters' rights were validated, the government filed an "ouster" suit. Some in the community thought Minerva should just walk away; others thought she should be compensated.

Townspeople, concerned for possible loss of the much-needed construction project, formed a committee to work out a compromise with the government. By act of Congress on June 10, 1930, Minerva was granted patent to the land, but then relinquished her rights. In return, carpenters and other workmen were to build her a home on land she had been willed by Mrs. Louise Fisher-Cole. In a column giving the Port Angeles community kudos for the accomplishments of 1933, the editor of the local newspaper specifically mentions the new Federal Building and Minerva's new house—"comfortable to the last detail." In a letter to the editor a livid Minerva responds with vitriol, "comfort is a thing unknown in this place." She goes on to detail her grievances—"no hot water, no functioning bath, no functioning electrical outlets and a flooded basement." Later in 1934 after major issues had been addressed and Minerva's temper had cooled, she completed her move.

Minerva was then joined by her mother in the new home, where she had her piano, her mementos, her painting and her china kiln. Upon her mother's death in 1935, Minerva painted a copy of *Saint Cecelia at the Organ* and presented it to St. Andrew's Episcopal Church as a memorial. Minerva's best paintings are her oils, which exhibit richness of color and depth of subject matter handled in a serious manner with a European look. She showed the least skill in handling portraits, although she said she especially liked to paint Eskimos, Orientals and Indians. The Indians reminded her of her youth when she had her own canoe to paddle about in the harbor. Minerva was a member of Seattle's first art organization and exhibited her work there twice.

Club work kept her busy: Daughters of the American Revolution, P.E.O., and the American Legion. As a founding member and one of the early presidents of the Clallam County Historical Society, she contributed many valuable photographs and other artifacts to its collections.

In 1954 Minerva suffered a stroke but she continued to teach and paint with the help of nurse-housekeepers. One of the women who helped care for Minerva tells of a New York couple, who after seeing Minerva's work asked her to do a large painting of the image on the Liberty Bond. Her friend and caretaker marveled at her ability to do this sepia tone oil painting larger than she was.

Another caretaker recalls how the Kallang painting, which had figured prominently in Minerva's youth, was rescued from the Roosevelt School boiler room. Minerva repaired the ornate gilded frame. Today, the painting hangs in the old Clallam County Courthouse. Her last painting of Jacob Hall, Chief White Feather of the Jamestown-Klallams, is owned by the Sequim-Dungeness Museum.

Minerva Troy was not the first lady of Port Angeles; that distinction goes to Caroline Smith. However, she was the community's first woman artist and no woman before or since exerted the all-around impact on Port Angeles that Minerva Troy did until her death in 1960.

Dr. Freeborn Stanton Lewis: The Infidel

Minerva Troy's father, Dr. Freeborn Stanton Lewis, served not only as the Puget Sound Cooperative Colony's medical officer but was a driving force philosophically in the colony. He was an editor of the colony's newspaper and the president of the "Infidels Club," a well-organized antireligious organization devoted to keeping religious activities out of the Port Angeles area. Dr. Lewis's efforts in this regard were seriously undermined by the dramatic conversion of one of the club's most dedicated members. The Methodist Episcopal Church in Port Angeles was thus born. The Infidel Club survived only into the mid-1890s; however, Dr. Lewis's influence in the area continued. The doctor was a three-term mayor of Port Angeles.

Wedding dress. Circa 1900
Forks Timber Museum Collection

Frontier Firebrand:
Caroline Jones Rixon

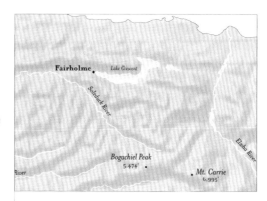

Caroline Jones was a woman who meticulously covered her back trail. She was obsessive in the destruction of clues to her past. Her parentage, date and place of birth are not known although local legend says she arrived at Lake Crescent in 1893 coming from California. Carrie and her soon-to-be ex-husband took up a homestead at the west end of the lake naming the site Fairholme. According to Carrie's granddaughter Polly Polhamus, after the property was proved up, "she divorced the guy and kicked him out and she kept the homestead." Carrie was always able to deal with a little breakage or collateral damage in the execution of her plans.

Carrie's stamina and success as a settler at this lonely location reveals as much about her early training as it does her character. It must be concluded that at some point early on Carrie's training deviated from the traditional to include axemanship, marksmanship, basic carpentry, small and large game hunting skills, and self-defense. These were skills she honed as she maintained her homestead, carried mail and supplies fourteen miles across the lake, and provided meat for her table. Carrie was self-sufficient, independent and content to spend the Gay 90s in her ivy-covered cabin six miles from the nearest neighbor—Mother

Editors Note:

High in the Olympics, in the ethereal company of Icarus, Aries, Mercury, Poseidon, Prometheus, Atlas, Aphrodite and Athena, a mountain with the name of a mortal woman guards the western flank of the beautiful Bailey Range. Her north, east and west contours are cloaked in snowfield and glacier, while the alpine meadows to the south of her summit give way to the rainforest of the Hoh River Valley.

The "best" approach to the mountain is across the length of a rocky knife-edged ridge aptly named, "the catwalk." Those who manage "the catwalk" enter a sacred realm of Native tradition and mythology with an unlikely name—Mount Carrie. The stories of this place are well known. It was to these heights the Klallams fled during the Great Flood and it was at a campsite that bears his name that Boston Charlie, the last shaman of the Klallams came for solitude and visions. But what about the mountain's name? Who was Carrie? The story of Carrie Jones Rixon is drawn from the historical record and an interview with Polly Polhamus (granddaughter of Carrie) conducted by Jacilee Wray, Olympic National Park anthropologist. Please note the edge in Polly's voice when the subject is her grandmother. The truth about Carrie may lie somewhere between the charmingly independent and talented lady of local lore and the less flattering picture drawn at times by her granddaughter Polly.

Opposite: English gentleman and Frontier Firebrand: Theodore and Caroline Rixon. 1900.
Polhamus Collection.

Right: Young Carrie Jones.
Polhamus Collection.

Preceding pages:
Mrs. Theo. F. Rixon at her homestead, Fairholme.
Polhamus Collection.

Theodore Rixon: Olympic Explorer

With the eastern part of the American continent cut and logging already starting in the west, by the late 1880s the United States was looking into a future without forests. A conservation movement was thus born that resulted in the Forest Reserve Act of 1891 giving power to the President to set aside national forest lands. On February 22, 1897, President Grover Cleveland turned 2,168,320 acres of the Olympic Peninsula into forest reserve. A survey was ordered by the Department of the Interior. Henry Gannett, Chief Geographer of the U.S. Geological Survey, hired Theodore Rixon and Arthur Dodwell and led them to the top of Mount Eleanor in the Southeast Olympics. After directing the men's attention to an endless sea of ridges, peaks, snowfields and glaciers to the west and north, Gannett is quoted as saying, "There's your work—go to it."

Three years later Rixon and Dodwell and their four assistants returned to civilization, having topographically mapped 3,483 square miles of the roughest terrain of the Peninsula under the most inhospitable conditions. Rixon's cruise by species netted a volume of sixty-one billion board feet. Of the 2,882 square miles of merchantable timber surveyed, only sixteen had been logged. A monstrous timber empire had been revealed.

Theodore Rixon

Above: Rixon home, Westlands, on the Soleduck River. Bunny's playhouse far right. 1920s.
Polhamus Collection.

Right: Carrie's friend in the high country. *Polhamus Collection.*

Barnes. Her cabin was an island of civilization in a vast timbered wilderness and it is said "she always had a kind word and helpful hand for the pilgrims heading into the deep forest of the upper Soleduck" (Story of Port Angeles).

One day, in the fall of 1898, out of the mountains walked quite literally the man of her dreams. He was handsome, with the attire, manners and bearing of an English gentleman complete with dress shirt, tie, pipe and felt hat. He approached her while she cut firewood and introduced himself as Theodore Rixon, a government timber cruiser and surveyor. Theodore protested that "a woman should not have to cut firewood" and pitched in to help. Theodore and Carrie were simultaneously smitten. When Theodore returned to the mountains he chose the tallest and most beautiful unnamed summit he could find and called the peak "Carrie" for Caroline Jones. The couple married in 1899.

Polly's less romantic version of the story speaks to Carrie's single-minded determination to always get what she wanted. Polly says: "When Caroline made up her mind... that was about it, and boy was she determined to get him and she got him." Not long after their marriage the Rixons built a cottage on their Fairholme property and decorated it with the finest accessories and contemporary furnishings. A large bookcase dominated one wall and Carrie's beloved upright piano the opposite wall. Several years later, Theodore found an

1872–Daniel Pullen and Frank Balch come to Quillayute country and establish trading posts.

Living large at Fairholme. Rixon home. 1900. *Polhamus Collection*

anomaly in previous surveys of the Peninsula's coastline that had left a parcel on Teahwhit Head unsurveyed and unclaimed. The Rixons filed on the property, and then built a cabin overlooking Second Beach near La Push. With much of his survey work occurring on the West End the Rixons split their time between the two homes. Carrie learned Chinook and at Teahwhit increased her circle of friends to include local Native ladies.

In 1914 the Rixon's adopted their only child, Gertrude, also known as "Bunny." Again Polly tells the story:

She was from a big family in Port Angeles. And the mother died and the father just kind of pawned the kids off to whoever wanted them. My mother always said she didn't like growing up as an only child. But she always said that it wasn't the Rixons fault because they wanted to adopt two, another sister of my mother's. But the father wouldn't let the child be adopted by them. And so it was too bad. This Caroline Rixon was very much of a peculiar person. Like when she adopted my mother she said, "You're mine

and you don't talk to the rest of any of your family".

Soon after adopting Bunny* who was eight at the time, the Rixons moved to a large home on the Sol Duc River about eleven miles east of Forks. The home had been built by one of the companies Theodore worked for. They called it Westlands. The huge three-story-home was surrounded by landscaped grounds with a garden and huge lily pond, home to some very large fish. Amenities also included certain architectural features designed to frustrate revenuers and facilitate the safe, discreet storage of refreshments.

On the property a playhouse built for Bunny replicated the Westlands design. It had two rooms and running water. At Westlands Carrie provided the best of everything for her daughter, including the finest traditional British education money could buy at Glenn Lyon School in Victoria B.C. Carrie's grandchildren, Tom and Polly, were also educated in Victoria.

Reflecting on the past, Polly acknowledged her

1875–Jamestown established.

Above: Carrie Jones Rixon homestead, Fairholme, on Lake Crescent   *Polhamus Collection.*

Opposite: Mt. Carrie   *Polhamus Collection.*

grandmother's sacrifice but at the same time questioned her priorities:

I mean I talk nasty about Carrie, my grandmother. But she was the kind that she wanted the best for everybody; she wanted us to go to private schools and she was always pushing and always in there. And you know she worked hard to raise my mother and see that my mother went to private school... And we were there summers and everything... And we had everything in the world. My grandfather... He would say, "Here is the money, go do what you want." And she was going to be high class.

Carrie was able to completely fulfill her artistic aspirations only after she and Theodore moved to Port Angeles. There she found a kindred spirit and friend in artist, musician and patron of the arts, Minerva Troy. Carrie further developed her painting with encouragement from Minerva and the two performed music publicly.

Efforts to capture the essence of Carrie all ultimately come to naught. For historians her life is a puzzle with one third of the pieces missing. No matter how the remaining two-thirds are placed, no clear picture emerges. By Carrie's order we know nothing of her parents, early life, or young adulthood. Her woodsman skills, painting, piano, and singing abilities and talent come out of a void. She is at once reclusive and gregarious, secretive and public, simple and extravagant, kind and controlling, independent and domineering. Just who was Caroline Jones Rixon? Of one thing we can be sure. Carrie was without a doubt an untamed woman of the Olympic wilderness.

* There is much confusion over Gertrude "Bunny" in the historical record stemming from the fact that Gertrude married Robert Rixon, a distant cousin of Theodore. Many make the easy but wrong assumption that Robert is a son of Carrie and Theodore and Gertrude is their daughter-in-law.

Postscript: The editors of this book are actively soliciting information regarding the following person: *Myrtle Templin Vincent, born Kansas, 1870. Married Walt Ferguson Fall 1908 at Fairhome. Father—Isaac Newton Templin Mother—Elizabeth Stevenson.*

1878—Ford Family settles Upper Prairie. (Forks Prairie)

Laura Hall Peters:
Nineteenth-Century Radical Daughter

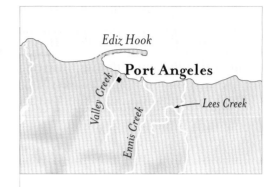

Laura Etta Crane Hall Peters was widely known in the last few decades of the 19th century because of her connection with major social reform movements: women's suffrage, temperance, Knights of Labor, Chinese expulsion, Populism, communitarianism, and spiritualism. Though there is a dearth of her own thought and ideas on record she was an active and often leading member of the organizations she chose to support.

Laura Hall Peters born in Fountain County, Indiana in 1840 was the fourth of five children of David and Catherine Rogers Crane. Her father could be termed "nomadic." He moved west from New Jersey to New York to Indiana to Iowa. The 1860 census reported his real estate assets worth about $2000.

In Iowa his daughter Laura met and married a dapper, young school teacher Isaac "Ike" Hall, who was the eldest of ten children in a family originally from Indiana. His father had been a skillful musician, a competent physician and a minister. The sons apparently shared their father's charisma. Ike's brother, Walter, married Laura's sister.

In 1864 wanderlust took over. Possibly David Crane shared the feelings of many of the men who were coming home from the Civil War; there must be something better, a fresh start further west. He and his wife moved about as far west as you could go. He went to work as a turner in Henry Yesler's saw mill and took advantage of opportunities to acquire land in Seattle. He owned some choice downtown business lots and built two expensive houses on Fourth Avenue which, before the great Seattle fire, was choice housing.

Ike and Laura started west with her parents, but stopped in San Francisco where her first child, a daughter Eudora, was born. In all, she would have three children—two daughters and a son.

They moved on to Seattle where Ike established himself as a lawyer and was admitted to the Territorial Bar. In his first case he defended two men accused of murder; his clients were convicted and sentenced to death by hanging. He

Above: Laura Peters
Opposite: Puget Sound Co–op. Colony Kindergarten at Ennis Creek (1st kindergarten). 1887.
Clallam County Museum Collection

Women's Suffrage in Washington

1854—Suffrage for women was defeated by the Territorial Legislature by one vote.

1883—A suffrage bill passed the legislature and women gained the right to vote.

1887—The Territorial Supreme Court ruled against women's suffrage. Women lost the right to vote.

1888—Another suffrage bill was passed only to be again overturned by the Court.

1910 An amendment to the Washington Constitution was passed giving women the right to vote.

apparently learned from that experience and was soon winning a reputation as a lawyer able to get his clients free on legal technicalities. Later he served as probate judge and even later as Seattle City Attorney. Within several years he was elected auditor—a position that made him principal administrative officer in King County at that time. Ike's career in law parallels that of other educated men who moved west. They read their Blackwell, put up a shingle as an attorney, developed a clientele and were admitted to the bar.

Ike's ambition did not stop at the legal profession. He was always alert to money- making opportunities and dabbled in newspapers. He produced several short-lived newspapers in Seattle supporting Union Republican principles. His friends rewarded Ike by nominating him for the position of auditor. He and another candidate tied. They drew straws and Mr. Hall was declared winner.

After almost a year he took a leave of absence to go to Hawaii, seeking other opportunities further west. Apparently his wife and two children were to follow him when the time was right.

While he was gone questions were raised about county accounting methods. Ike may have been incompetent (his compatriots agreed) but he was not a criminal. He came back from Hawaii, talked about settling in Port Townsend, but finally returned to Seattle for good. He dabbled in politics, embarked on another newspaper enterprise, and finally settled into a law practice.

Laura's life, during these unsettled times focused on her family. She was not much into housework-preferring writing and painting to dusting and cooking. The story is told that on occasion, Ike, fed up with lack of good housekeeping and good meals, took his daughter to a hotel or restaurant for a large dinner. A granddaughter later reported, "with all the desserts they liked best first."

During this time Laura was not apparently interested or involved in her husband's newspapers. Her first reform cause was temperance. Before 1870 she was an officer with the first Seattle Lodge of the Independent Order of Good Templars (a temperance organization). She helped organize

Puget Sound Colony gardens. Late 1880.

Clallam County Museum Collection

1882—Shaker Church established in South Sound.

1883—A suffrage bill passed the legislature and women gained the right to vote.

the second Templar Lodge in Seattle. Later she was nominated, but not elected, to the highest position a woman could hold in the state Templar organization. At first Ike joined Laura in the temperance movement, but he soon became known for his heavy drinking and ability to hold his liquor. It was said that he often went into court "falling down drunk" but able to think clearly and win clearly. It was then that his renowned wit was especially evident.

In 1874 Laura filed for divorce, charging that he was an habitual drunkard who went on sprees that lasted several weeks. He neglected his family, she stated, and threatened her at those times. The court talked them into reconciliation and the marriage lasted nine more years. The third child, Luella, was born during that time.

In 1883 Laura went to court again. This time there was no reconciliation and the marriage was dissolved.

Laura found herself on the fringe of the best society in frontier Seattle. Divorce was fairly common in Seattle in those years. Doc Maynard, one of the major leading early figures in Seattle history, had walked down the main street with "a wife on each arm" before persuading the Territorial Legislature to grant him a divorce from his first wife whom he had abandoned when he left for the western states. However, it was easier for a divorced man to win society's acceptance than for a woman.

When Laura looked for a way to regain her status, and to keep busy, she became involved in the activities for which we recognize her place in history.

Her interest in women suffrage began about the time her marriage began to fall apart. In 1871 Laura had been one of the Washington residents who heard Susan B. Anthony talk about the merits of giving women the right to vote. Laura signed up to sponsor an equal suffrage convention in Olympia and was appointed to the constitution committee. The campaign was successful in 1883 when women in Washington Territory won the right to vote. Laura was on the first mixed jury in King County in 1883. The right to vote was overturned by the Territory Supreme Court in 1887- Judge Turner presiding. Laura was

First Puget Sound Co-op building. 1887. port Angeles, Washington
Clallam County Museum Collection

1887–The Territorial Supreme Court ruled against women's suffrage.
Women lost the right to vote.

among the protesters and even paid to have a pro-women suffrage petition printed. A public meeting was planned. Women received the right to vote again in 1888 but lost the right with statehood in 1889. It was not written into the state constitution.

In the early 1890s, the Equal Suffrage Association was organized and Laura became vice president. The Populists kept their promise to pass an equal suffrage bill and Laura was appointed by the Association to lobby the bill through both houses. When the bill was finally passed, Laura was sworn in as a special messenger and personally carried the bill to Governor John R. Rogers to sign. In the state's November elections the amendment was defeated. Some blame a lack of unity on the part of the state suffrage organization—a leadership fight between members on the east and west sides of the state.

Suffrage and temperance were not Laura's only interests. In the mid-1880s she joined the Knights of Labor (one of the first successful labor unions). The Knights advocated equality of sexes, as well as cooperative institutions and government ownership of utilities. The Knights were organizing women, as well as wage earners, professional people, farmers, etc. Her father, son and nephew, who were printers, belonged to unions. At that time a cousin, Peter P. Goode, who had lived for a time in a French Co–op, arrived in Seattle and the two seemed to mutually support each other in reform activities.

The Knights were heavily involved in the anti-Chinese activities of this period. Chinese laborers had been imported into the Pacific Northwest and California to build the transcontinental railroads. After the railroads were built, they moved into the cities where they provided a source of cheap labor. The Knights saw them as a threat—displacing white workers. The Knight newspaper, *The Daily Call*, edited by Laura's son and nephews, was emphatic in insisting "The Chinese Must Go." Vigilantes went from house to house in the Chinatown sections of Seattle and Tacoma, rounded up all the Chinese they could find and escorted them to the waterfront where they forced several ship captains to take as many on board as they could and sail away from the town. There were more Chinese on the dock than there was room on the ships in port so those remaining were kept guarded on an open dock in traditional damp

November Seattle weather for several days. The Governor intervened by declaring martial law and sent in the National Guard to disperse the crowd and escort the remaining Chinese back to their homes.

Laura's father was heavily involved in the pro-labor Liberal League and active in the anti-Chinese movement, although not involved in the riots. He chaired meetings, signed a bond to guarantee ship passage for some of the Chinese and eventually testified for the defense. Mr. Crane was propertied, but he had never identified with the landed leaders in Seattle, being something of a rebel. He supported suffrage for women, unionism and other interests which were concerns of his daughter. Later a writer claimed that the anti-Chinese demonstrations brought out "every long-haired man and short-haired woman." Laura and her father were among those he was referring to.

Laura's cousin, Peter Goode, also worked in the anti-Chinese movement. He was a visionary who spoke of building a model city where people would be equal and would work cooperatively.

An attorney who had moved to Seattle from San Francisco, George Venable Smith, was also active in the Chinese expulsion. Smith, Goode and Laura exchanged ideas for a utopian society and on the death of Goode, (possibly caused by an illness contracted when he was imprisoned for his anti-Chinese activities) Smith adopted the idea and founded the Puget Sound Cooperative Colony with himself as President and Laura Hall the only woman on the Board of Directors. Laura was elected corresponding secretary of the corporation and education director. The Colony started a newspaper, *The Model Commonwealth* and Laura became the first editor. The motto of the newspaper was "Let the many combine in co-operation as the few have done in corporations." Although most of the newspaper was devoted to reprints from other Utopian communities (there were eight or nine in Washington Territory alone) it is believed that she wrote the fillers urging readers to rise above human nature and pushing the idea that the poor had nothing to lose and everything to gain by joining the Colony. She wrote a column directed at children and wrote the Colony's view of women: "We are, as colonists, equal with our brother." Equal suffrage and equal pay were promised. Cooperative kitchens would solve the problem of hiring servants to cook. No one would work for another person. Women like Laura, who did not like to cook, could work in other activities and leave the cooking to those women whose interests and contributions lay in those areas.

Laura also appreciated the Colony idea of religion. There would be no churches. Some believe that the "good moral people of Seattle" shunned Laura after her divorce. At any rate, after her divorce she dropped out of the church choir in which she had been a leading voice, stopped going to church and adopted spiritualism.

The colony moved to Port Angeles in 1887 and that spring Laura and her youngest daughter Luella made the move. The colony was located in East Port Angeles, along Ennis Creek. Some lived in tent cabins. Other shared space in two wooden, two- story hotels. That September opposition arose to Smith's leadership and elections were held. The colonists in Port Angeles voted mainly against Smith, but proxies from the many colony supporters who still lived elsewhere, poured in and Smith and his board were reelected.

Shortly after that Laura resigned her editorship. *The Model Commonwealth* continued to exist for several more years under other editors. It became a truly radical publication. At one time bold print under the mast head declared: Free Land and Free Love. Another time it expressed support for the leaders of the Haymarket Riot in Chicago with a black border around the article telling about the atrocities.

Laura continued to serve as Education Director. One of the people she corresponded with while promoting the colony was a man named Charles J. Peters, a Swiss immigrant twelve years younger than she, who had settled in Fort Worth, Texas. Peters, starry-eyed about the democratic ideals of the movement, joined the Cooperative Colony and moved to Port Angeles shortly after Laura arrived. He worked on *The Model Commonwealth* for a while but apparently became disillusioned with the actuality of the situation and bought land west of the Port Angeles reserve and put together a large farm.

On May 21, 1888, he and Laura were married "in the open air at Port Angeles" by William Burch, a justice of the peace. They honeymooned in Europe where Charles showed off his bride to his family and returned to Port Angeles. Laura and Charles took part in cultural events in west Port

Angeles near Peabody Creek. She enjoyed singing and Laura and her daughter probably appeared in local theatricals in the Opera House. She sang the Star Spangled Banner in one of the first Fourth of July celebrations.

In 1893 Laura's husband served as the Clallam County Commissioner for the Chicago World's Fair Commission in Washington State. Laura helped. The two probably helped raise much of the money to pay for the painting of the Port Angeles Harbor that now hangs in the Courthouse stairwell. Laura continued her interest in the temperance movement. An active chapter developed. She also continued to work for women's suffrage.

In the 1890s Laura adopted the Populism Movement and in 1896 when the Populists, Democrats and Silver Republicans met in a "Fusion Convention" in Ellensburg, Washington, Laura was a member of the Clallam County Populist delegation and the only woman delegate present. Her interest was in writing a woman suffrage plank in the Populist Party platform. The party endorsed the plank, but their candidate for governor, John R. Rogers did not mention it in his inaugural address. In spite of that she supported Governor Rogers and took part in a campaign to get the legislature to raise the age of consent for women.

Laura died in 1902 after a lengthy illness. She is remembered as the central and moving spirit of the Colony. She was aggressive, progressive, strong and positive in her convictions. Laura was plain in manner and dress. Living in a time of great social change, Laura's motif was that of equality, especially as it related to women. Although Laura Etta Crane Hall Peters is barely known in the pages of popular Washington history, she witnessed and participated in a time of intense ideas and activities, a time when many of the institutions we take for granted in the 21st century germinated and took root.

Life on the Home Front: A Civil War Soldier's Wife's Reflections

Esther Ford - Age 16. 1856.

Sharon Nilsen Collection

I am not going to state the cause of the Rebellion, it would take too much time. It lasted four years from April 12, 1861 to the surrender of General Lee's army April 9, 1865. My husband enlisted at Warsaw, Indiana in the 4th Regiment Co. B. Indiana Cavalry for three years or as long as the war lasted. He saw three years of active service.

I was to tell you how the women had to get along. Well, we had a hard time of it. I was left with a little baby four weeks old to care for. I lived with my sister-in-law the first year, then she went to her brother in Wisconsin. Then I was left all alone with my baby and I suffered much with fear and anxiety not knowing what might happen. I had to get and chop my own wood the best I could. When I could do no better I took the rails from the fence and chopped them up to burn. There was no man to haul a stick of wood. I had a small patch of potatoes and some other vegetables. I had a cow and some chickens and made my own butter and cheese.

I lived on a farm and there were no near neighbors or a woman whom I could go to see for a few minutes. It took all the able-bodied men during the four years from the farms and shops. Lawyer, doctors, preachers and merchants all enlisted and went to carry a gun at thirteen dollars a month not because they wanted to but for the love of their country and pay. The industries of the country were at a stand still. The women did not do much cooking as there was not much to cook. It did not cost much to get women to conserve food that would sustain life; they learned that by hard experience after the men were gone.

The women planted the corn and potatoes and harvested them with their own hands. They raised chickens, pigs and cattle. I have forgotten what the price of beef and pork were. I know it was very high but I remember after the war was over and Mr. Ford came home, he bought a pig for our winter meat. I think it weighed 150 pounds. He paid thirty-five dollars for it. Cotton goods were very high in price. Common muslin one yard wide was sixty cents a yard, calico was thirty and forty cents a yard and very hard to get at that price....

When Mr. Ford had been gone about a year his company was taken as prisoners and used in exchange for other prisoners whom our men had taken and kept as prisoners in Indianapolis, Indiana. They sent the Union men to be exchanged for their prisoners. When they got to Indianapolis, Mr. Ford telegraphed for me to come and see him. Some of the other women, whose husbands were there, went too. We stayed a few days or until they were exchanged.

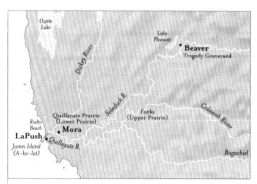

Some time after this Mr. Ford was taken sick and they gave him a furlough to come home for two weeks. When the time was up he was so weak that the doctor reported him not able to go but as soon as he was able to walk with a cane he was ordered back to Indianapolis. That tries the heart of a woman when she sees her husband going away when she does not know if she will ever see him again alive.

I had an old uncle and aunt who lived about three miles from where I did who gave my baby and me a home during the rest of the war. I worked hard to pay for our board while there. There were no nurses to take care of the sick and wounded as there are now. The women volunteered to go as nurses to care for the wounded and sick. There were five hundred nurses registered on the Government rolls. They had no white caps and their dresses were mostly blue calico and gingham aprons. Some had their hair cut short like the men.

E.A. Ford

Editor's Note:

Luther Ford, Esther, his wife and two of their children were the first family to settle Forks Prairie. In this letter, written after their move to Quillayute country, Esther recalls the tribulations of a young soldier's wife.

Ford farmhouse - Forks. 1900.

1888—Another suffrage bill was passed only to be again overturned by the Court.

PAGE 69

Winifred "Mamie" Ford Peterson
Dangerous Crossing

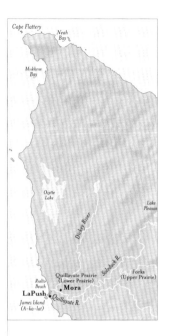

I was born in Iowa in 1866. My father, Luther M. Ford, who had fought with the Federal troops during the Civil War, had returned from service in ill health. In 1870 he moved with my family to Florida, in the hope that the warmer climate of the state would be beneficial. But in place of the deep black soil and friendly neighborliness of Iowa, he found only sand and "no welcome at all for a Northerner," for this was the day of the carpetbaggers. We tried for a number of years to find a suitable home, living for a time in Kansas, and later in California.

In the latter state, at San Diego, my father was attracted by stories of opportunity and a healthful climate in Washington and in 1877 brought his family northward to Seattle. Seattle at that time consisted only of a few houses huddled along the waterfront, with a settler here and there farther inland. My father had an opportunity to buy 80 acres of timbered land in what is now the heart of downtown Seattle for $400, but he decided against it and set out with my family for La Push, intending to take a claim somewhere inland from the mouth of the Quillayute. A small schooner carried the family and their effects to Neah Bay, from which small settlement we had expected to continue my journey by Indian canoe. But heavy weather kept the family from making the start, for even the Indians, who were expert canoe men, feared to attempt passage around Cape Flattery

We lived in Neah Bay in what had been originally a fort or blockhouse, and later a school for six weeks. On January 1, 1878, unwilling to wait longer, with the aid of some Indian guides and packers, we made our way by trail and water from Neah Bay to Mukkaw Bay on the Pacific coast, following a small stream to the Waach River, and thus avoiding the dangers attendant upon an attempted passage around the cape. In Mukkaw Bay we loaded our few household goods, clothing, tools and provisions into one large ocean canoe manned by five Indian paddlers and, together with Dan Pullen (another settler) entered another Indian oared canoe and started for the mouth of the Quillayute.

Although our start from Mukkaw Bay had seemed propitious, the canoes had not gone far until stormy weather was again encountered, and it was decided to keep as close to shore as the surf would permit. But somewhere along the coast, wind and tide carried the canoes among rocks and reefs upon which breakers pounded so terrifyingly that even the Indians, experienced though they were, lost heart and made ready to die. They laid down their paddles and began to chant a death song. But Pullen and my parents were unwilling to die without at least making an effort to escape the sea. After much argument and encouragement they induced the Indians to take up their paddles again and make one more attempt to pull away from the dangerous rocks. A short time later both canoes were safely out in the ocean.

Editor's Note:

January 1, 1878, Winifred Ford, second daughter of Luther and Esther, made the trip from Neah Bay to LaPush with her sister and parents. In this 1936 interview with Gilbert Pilcher, Winifred tells the story of this perilous winter voyage down a stormy Pacific Coast.

Opposite: Winifred Ford Peterson and Ely Peterson in an official wedding portrait.

Right: back side of the portrait with names and a date, September 23, 1882.
Peterson Collection

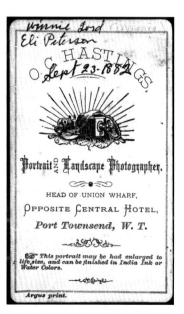

Inventory of goods shipped from Winnie Peterson visiting in Seattle to husband Ely Peterson in Forks.

Posted in letter dated Dec. 28, 1895

5 pair of shoes

7 pair of stockings

7 pair of overalls

1 blanket

2 towels

2 pieces of gingham

2 pieces of muslin

3 overshirts

2 suits of underwear

4 pair of drawers

7 shirts for boys

3 hats

5 packages of tacks

1 package of birdseed

1 lamp and lantern wick

4 lbs of Battle-axe Tobacco

1 revolver

2 whistles

4 handkerchiefs

2 ribbons

2 pair of suspenders

1 package of writing paper

firecrackers

My sister, too young to appreciate the danger, lay in the bottom of the canoe, covered with blankets and our faces and our hair were wet from the spray that broke over the canoe's side. We were not afraid; rather, we enjoyed the experience, and the songs of the Indians charmed us. Although I cannot remember clearly, I believe the Indians were singing hymns taught them previously by missionaries, rather than their own cruder songs; for I can clearly recall that the Ayres were of the same type as old-time church songs.

All through the night the Indians paddled, and at four o'clock in the morning we reached safety behind a sand spit at the mouth of the Quillayute river. The next day was spent in transporting our goods to safe ground on Quillayute Prairie; and here Mother and we girls remained for several days, in a deserted cabin, while my father and Mr. Pullen scouted through the brush and timber for a location.

Life on the Prairie

My father laid claim to 160 acres of open prairie a mile from the present site of Forks, and with the aid of friendly Indians, our goods were brought up the Quillayute and Calawah rivers to a point two miles from the claim, and from there packed in on the backs of the settlers. Shelter was soon set up, and then a log house built. Very early in the spring, potatoes were planted and every effort made to provide food from the land. Elk, deer and bear supplied meat in plenty. As soon as the small family was fairly settled, father went back to Seattle to bring

Opposite page: Winifred Ford Peterson. Late 1870s. *Peterson Collection*

Below: Quileute Women's Dance. Peterson house in far background. 1900s.
Peterson Collection

1889—Land boom sweeps Port Angeles waterfront. In one year population grows from 500 to 3000.

out some cattle. These were carried by schooner to La Push and driven up along the rivers to the homestead. The Ford place, unlike most homesteads, was virtually all prairie, and the family found it easier to begin at once to earn a living from the land, for no time had to be wasted in clearing. As soon as crops of hay, grain and vegetables began to appear, other needed supplies could be obtained by barter. There was little money in circulation, but always a way, it seemed to obtain the necessities of life. Most of the clothing worn by us was made by mother from calico obtained from the Indians, through a decidedly roundabout method. The Indians would trade furs or fish at the trading post for calicos, which they would then exchange to the settlers for fresh vegetables, eggs, homemade cheese, etc.

I was married at the age of 16 to Ely Peterson, who was at that time 28, and who had settled on a claim adjoining that of the Fords. At 17, I became the first school teacher in the Forks district, holding the school sessions in my home. Only a three month's term was provided for and pupils ranged in age from five to eighteen years. Reading, writing, arithmetic, grammar and geography were included in the curriculum. Mail for the settlers on Forks prairie was brought by canoe from Neah Bay to La Push when possible; when the waves were too dangerous, the trip was made along the beach. The first trails were those made by bands of elk, and gradually widened by slashing. Along these trails were many great logs—wind-fallen trees—and steps were cut into the sides of some so that the settlers could step over them more easily. Even the ponies later learned to put their hoofs into these steps and climb over windfalls five or six feet in diameter. For a time only three other settlers were located near our place. We were permitted to go to La Push once or twice a year, and in following the trails frequently had to ford many streams or cross them on foot logs when not fordable. My father died in 1907; my mother in 1932. I have been a widow for some years. My home, and that of my brother Ollie Ford, who lives on the original Ford homestead, are veritable museums of relics of olden times, and contain many fine elk head, cougar and bear skins and mounted birds.

From: *Clallam County Washington Pioneers*
Gilbert Pilcher

1889—Quileute Reservation is established by President Cleveland's executive order.

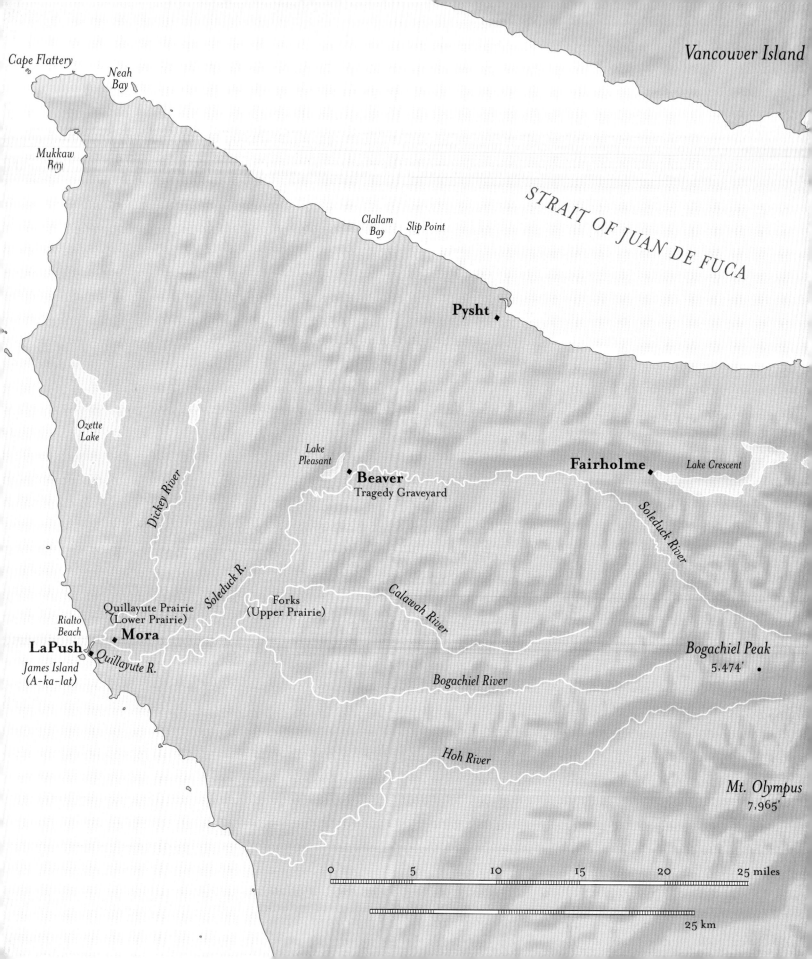

Vancouver Island

Cape Flattery

Neah
Bay

Mukkaw
Bay

STRAIT OF JUAN DE FUCA

Clallam
Bay   Slip Point

Pysht ◆

Ozette
Lake

Dickey River

Lake
Pleasant

Beaver ◆
Tragedy Graveyard

Fairholme ◆   Lake Crescent

Soleduck River

Soleduck R.

Calawah River

Forks
(Upper Prairie)

Quillayute Prairie
(Lower Prairie)

Rialto
Beach

LaPush ◆   **Mora**
◆ Quillayute R.

James Island
(A-ka-lat)

Bogachiel River

Bogachiel Peak
5,474' ◆

Hoh River

Mt. Olympus
7,965'

0   5   10   15   20   25 miles

25 km

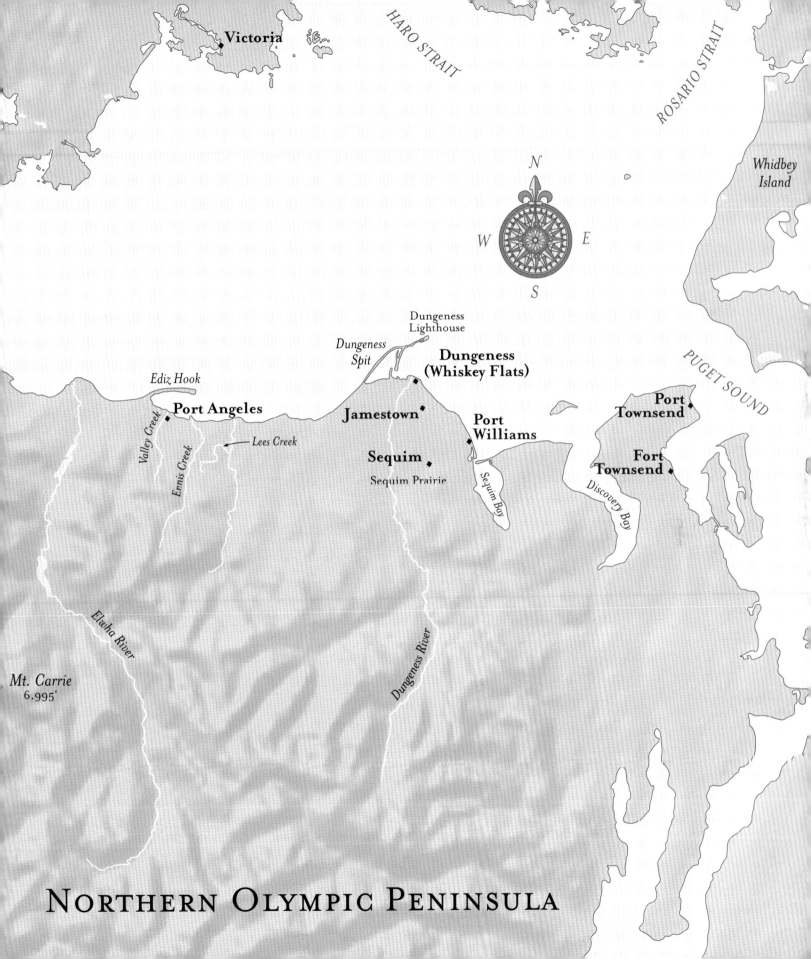

HARO STRAIT

ROSARIO STRAIT

Victoria

Whidbey Island

N

W   E

S

PUGET SOUND

Dungeness
Lighthouse

Dungeness Spit

Dungeness (Whiskey Flats)

Ediz Hook

Port Angeles

Jamestown

Port Williams

Port Townsend

Valley Creek

Ennis Creek

Lees Creek

Sequim

Sequim Prairie

Sequim Bay

Fort Townsend

Discovery Bay

Elwha River

Mt. Carrie
6,995'

Dungeness River

NORTHERN OLYMPIC PENINSULA

Karl Fisher ranch, Hoh Valley   *Clallam County Museum Collection*

Klootchman on the Warpath or
"How Two-Hat Fisher Got His Name"

North of the Upper Hoh road in Western Jefferson County, at a point just beyond the Hell Roaring Creek Crossing, hand-split cedar remnants of the old pioneer puncheon trail are barely visible. One hundred years ago when this trail was in good repair, it could be followed east about seven miles to the homestead of Karl Fisher.

Karl arrived in the Hoh Valley in the 1890s and it was not long before he realized the need to diversify his agricultural enterprise. He built some trail and did a little trapping but found his gift in the beverage-making business. Not a man to waste any time pursuing his calling, Karl set about in a most ambitious manner to meet a robust, growing demand for his product. Since remote West End Jefferson County had always existed in a state of benign neglect, Karl never lost any sleep over fear of official sanction. Furthermore, since he was already routinely breaking at least a half dozen federal and state laws, the fact that Karl also frequently violated the prohibition against selling liquor to Indians never weighed very heavily on his mind.

So it was that when two thirsty braves and their klootchman arrived at his cabin one fall during cranberry season, Karl did not hesitate to accommodate the wishes of the braves. While the women toiled in the bogs on the south side of the Hoh, the braves occupied themselves with a fresh batch of Karl's hooch. Karl, it seems, also had a little bit just to be sociable, then took a nap. Several hours later he awoke abruptly after being set upon by the two klootchman; both were screaming like banshees as they completed the grizzly task of separating Karl from his scalp. Their shrieks and Karl's shouts finally woke the braves. When the klootchman discovered that Karl had not killed their husbands as they had assumed, they ceased their murderous efforts. However, Karl's disfigurement was complete and from that time on he wore a skull cap under his crusher and was known as Two-Hat Fischer.

Credit for story—Missy Barlow

1889—Native village at LaPush burns.

Allen Weir's description of pioneer life

Saluda Jane Buchanan Weir, cousin of President James Buchanan and wife of John Weir, was born in Alabama and came to Dungeness Country in 1860 by way of Texas, the Santa Fe Trail and California. Saluda was a deeply religious, fearless, frontier woman who was as comfortable sewing buckskin clothing for her family as she was rallying temperance troops. The typical sixties home Saluda's son, Allen, describes is in all likelihood his own. Note the fun Allen has with frontier dialect.

Houses were most built of logs, with clapboard roof and clay fireplaces. When Captain McAlmond built one of real lumber throughout, actually lathed and plastered, with real boughten doors and a cornice around the roof, there was a general feeling that the country had taken a long stride towards the opulence and luxury of the Old World. The Captain was elected justice of the peace out of pure deference for his superior attainments.

The Dungeness people enjoyed life, however, after a fashion. Carpets for their floors were entirely unknown and only the upper 10 could afford chairs with rawhide bottoms. The others had to worry along with wooden benches and stools; and very little time was wasted, either in vain regrets or longings for more luxuries.

Each house had its big, open fireplace in the largest living room, and that fireplace, if it was the regulation size, would accommodate a four-foot backlog.

Against that backlog would be built a fire to correspond

in size and heat with the severity of the weather. Long winter evenings would be spent by the family in front of the fire. If there was a bearskin rug in front of the hearth for the smaller children to play on they were happy and contented.

The older members of the household would play fox-and-geese or read the newspapers if there happened to be any. The men would load their pipes and perhaps spin yarns about the most remarkable of their injun fights on the plains or maybe they would tell the wonder-eyed youngsters about the ole Missoury or Kentuck or Eelynoy or they would speculate as to whether or not Abe Lincoln could lick them there Southerners, or, dropping into reminiscent mood, would tell of corn-husking with the boys and gals 30 years ago.

There was very little in the surroundings to inspire a poetic or sentimental tendency. It was mostly hard, stern reality. The neighborhood "shindig," Fourth of July horse races and Sunday afternoon poker games constituted the main part of the diversion.

The Superintendent:
Ina May Agnew

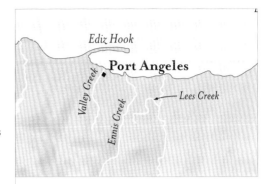

Ina May Agnew was born into a pioneer homesteading family that predated the Puget Sound Co-operative Colony, but ties to the colony were strong. She was born to Charles and Sarah Morse Agnew on May 10, 1880, at a Lees Creek homestead east of Port Angeles. Her parents separated when she was young, and she and her mother lived with her grandparents, Caroline and Alfred Lee, and her young uncle and aunt, Oscar and Ida Lee. The Lee farm was located on what the settlers called Mount Misery (later changed to Mount Pleasant).

In a diary kept during her eighth year, Ina recorded the events of daily life on a homestead. Her entries tell a tale of neighborly interdependence in isolated, undeveloped country. The colony's purchases of beef, butter, potatoes, and other produce from homesteaders such as the Lees helped keep settlers going. The colony's social life, including its dances, helped break down the isolation. But to Ina, its school was most important. Once the colony built the town's Central School at First and Vine, Ina completed her education there, graduating in 1897.

Ina Agnew on far right. Late 1890s. Newly minted teachers at Ellensberg Normal School. *John McNutt Collection*

1891–Port Angeles Opera House built.

That fall, Ina taught school at Dry Creek, starting a career that would end with her retirement in 1944. She attended Ellensburg Normal School for a year between teaching jobs. In 1899, she met Harland P. McNutt, a new arrival from Nova Scotia. The teacher and the blacksmith were married November 7, 1900, at Port Angeles. Tragedy entered their lives in 1907, when their infant daughter Carolyn died.

Early on Ina set her sights on a leadership role in education. She had been teaching at her alma mater, Central School, when she was elected Clallam County Superintendent of Schools in 1911. The letters published here were written during this first two-year term. She then took time out to have two sons, Harlan in 1914 and Oscar in 1917. She was elected county superintendent once again in 1919 for a four-year term. During this time, her marriage to McNutt ended and she married Leonard Olson. Her career in administration continued with service as deputy county superintendent of schools in Snohomish, Skagit and Clallam counties. She then returned to teaching and at the time of her retirement was teaching at Washington School in Port Angeles. Ina lived at her home on Lees creek until her death in 1965.

One of the duties of a county superintendent of schools early in this century was to visit every school in the county at least once during the year to examine facilities and teachers' techniques. Two months after taking over as Clallam County superintendent of school in September 1911, the conscientious Ina McNutt set out with her husband Harland to fulfill her obligation to visit schools in the West End. Letters she wrote to her aunt, Mrs. J.O. (Ida Lee) Morse of Port Angeles describe the challenges of reaching the isolated homestead schools.

Previous pages: Ina and companion out for a drive.

John McNutt Collection

Clallam Bay
November 11, 1911

Dear Ida,

We are still alive but that's about all. This is the worst I ever imagined. I wrote you Monday night and told you all the news up to that time. Well, Tuesday morning we saddled the horses and started over the Tyee Mountain to Nels Nelson's (on Hoko River). It poured rain and the trail was the worst I ever saw. The trail to the mountains back of Port Angeles is a boulevard beside it. It took us about four hours to make seven miles. We expected to go back to Sappho that night but Nelson told us we had better go from his place into Dickey Lake and the Ozette country. He said it would save us a good many miles, so we decided to stay at his place all night and go to Dickey Lake the next day. Well, the next morning we got up real early so as to get a good start and imagine our surprise when we found it snowing hard. We started anyway and Nelson went with us to the Hoko River to show us where to ford. The river was very high. We almost had to swim the horses. We got to (John) Sand's place about 11:30. By this time an awful wind had come up and it was hailing. The hail stones would almost cut your face. I visited the (Dickey Lake) school, had dinner and then we made another start for the Ozette country. The trail was awful. We were afraid we would lose the horses, and the wind was blowing a gale. You can imagine how we felt going through that timber in a wind storm and the Hoko River to ford and it was a raging torrent.

We got as far as (Inger) Klaboe's that night and stayed all night. The next morning we started for Ozette Lake. Another awful trail. The wind still blowing and it would snow while and then hail. The last five miles of the trail was so bad the people told us we would be foolish to try to take the horses over it, so we left them in an old barn and got a fellow to take us over to the school in a launch. The launch was just an old patched up canoe with an engine in it and the lake was awful rough. I was just scared to death. I tell

1892—John Huelsdonk, "Iron Man of the Hoh," settles Upper Hoh River

Above: Ina at one of her early teaching assignments in Clallam County. 1900.
John McNutt Collection

1893–Panic of 1893 grips country. First National Bank of Port Angeles closes
doors wiping out savings of many.

PAGE 83

Ina McNutt (fourth from right) watching bone games at Neah Bay. 1910s.

John McNutt Collection

you I was glad when we got back to the horses. We stayed all night at Ole H. Boe's. He is a bachelor and just he and his mother live together. That night it turned colder and all the water in our bedroom froze solid. I visited the Royal School that morning then we started over the Hoko trail to Clallam. We arrived here yesterday about four o'clock. I was nearly frozen stiff. The trail was full of slides and we had a terrible time getting around. The horses had snow-balls on their feet and it was dangerous to ride for fear they would slip and go into the river. I walked about half way and Harlan walked nearly all the way. I certainly was glad to get to this hotel. We thought of going to Sappho today but it was so bad over the mountain that we couldn't very well make it. Our rig is at Sappho. If it moderates tomorrow we will try to make it. It had been snowing here all day. I guess the worst of our trip is over, at least I hope so. In most of the districts I visited they told me a

Superintendent had never been in and I don't wonder at it. There is about ten inches of snow here now. There was over a foot when we left Royal yesterday. If it continues snowing we may come home without going any farther.

Tuesday morning, 8:30

Sappho
November 14, 1911

Dear Ida,

Well, we are still alive and both feeling well. We are starting for Forks this morning. I shall visit three schools on the way. The snow is nearly all gone. We rode in from Clallam yesterday. It poured all the way. It took us five hours for the roads were very bad. If we have good luck we will probably be home a week from next Friday. Love to all.

Ina

1897—Olympic Forest Reserve established by President Cleveland

Ella Guptill (center back row), daughter of sea captain H.M. and Mary Guptill, came to Port Angeles with her family in 1888. Education and the arts were important to the Guptill family. Ella's brother Tom was a poet and artist with an intense interest in the outdoors. Tom's manuscripts and sketches can be found in the archives of the Clallam County Museum, while many of his finished works are hidden under remodeled walls of older Port Angeles buildings.

Ella's interest tended more toward the philosophical. She was attracted to the Puget Sound Cooperative Colony by its utopian vision of equal rights for all and its promise of a worker's paradise.

Ella was hired to teach at the Colony School soon after her family's arrival in Port Angeles. The picture above was taken in March of 1889 during her first year of employment. By 1894 Ella was bringing home $55 a month from her job at the colony's new Central School. Although the colony was to fold a short time later, Ella continued to live by its principles. In November of 1894 she courted controversy by getting herself elevated to Clallam County Superintendent of Schools. Women in Washington had lost the right to vote with statehood in 1889 so her election was contested. The issue was settled for Ella and all women later in her term. It was decided lack of suffrage did not preclude holding the county school superintendent position. Ella further endeared herself to certain of her public by her vocal educational activism. In 1895, shortly after taking office, she wrote "... the Legislature has never made ample provision for our country schools, ...teachers are unable to make the schoolroom the place of active life training it should be, ...children leave school before they have even laid the foundation for education."

Ella Guptill (center, back row) taught more than 50 students of all ages at the Puget Sound Co-operative Colony School when this photograph was made about March 1889. Among her students was Ina Agnew (second row, second from left), who would grow up to follow in the footsteps of her teacher.

1900—Rixon and Dodwell complete Olympic Forest Reserve survey and timber cruise.

Deadly Deceptions

Few women dared brave the cold, wet climate and rugged terrain of the northern reaches of the Olympic Peninsula in the 1870s and `80s. It was largely a man's world and women were in shorter supply than sunshine in this relentlessly cloud-shrouded, rain drenched wilderness. Rarely did women venture into rugged frontier territory alone. On occasion prenuptial promises overcame primal fear and a man successfully persuaded his bride to accompany him to the wilderness. Such was the case when Mr. Brenton convinced his lovely bride, Rose, to set up housekeeping on the pristine shores of Lake Pleasant.

Bordered on the southwest side by a natural prairie, Lake Pleasant provided the early settlers an unspoiled backdrop for their homesteads. Several small cabins had been built around the lake including that of Chris Grauskrouse, a trapper, whose home was located at the north end or head of the lake. A man named Charley Paul lived on the east side in a small cabin near the shore. An otherwise decent looking fellow, Charley was blond, of medium build but was missing an eye. Children feared him and ran whenever he came around.

Across the lake from Charley's place lived Mr. Brenton with his attractive and charming wife, Rose. Their three-room, ivy-covered cabin had been built from hand-split cedar on a clearing close to the shore. Neighbors around the lake knew each other and even though most were self-sufficient, they often relied on each other to survive in this rough country. Certain resources were in short supply and neighbors were happy to share or help out with a hand to anyone in need. Women were the scarcest resource of all in this wild country but in this regard, Mr. Brenton wasn't generous. For her part, Rose could have used a female confidante and on many a long winter night, she felt the sting of loneliness known only too well by those who endured the emptiness of the frontier. Furthermore, Mr. Brenton's prenuptial promises had remained largely unfulfilled. By all accounts Rose Brenton was as feisty and spirited as she was beautiful, but this beauty had been plucked from a groomed landscape and replanted in the wild. The unrelenting loneliness of frontier life proved more difficult than she could have ever imagined. Rose welcomed any break in the monotony and eagerly opened her home to the lake residents. Sharing resources, however, got out of hand when Rose began distributing charm to receptive visitors. The attention she invited from the bachelors in the area provided some excitement, a little escape from the constant boredom. She was young and naïve and her charm attracted the attention of one particularly love-starved homesteader. Rose only meant to have a little fun.

But Charley was not just having fun; he was obsessed. He may have only had one eye but that eye was focused—on Rose. Charley had always been a patient man and he knew that to get what he wanted meant eliminating the only thing standing in his way—Rose's husband. He waited. Finally his patience paid off. When Rose left to visit relatives in Seattle, Charley Paul made his move.

Perhaps Mr. Brenton had suspicions about his wife's relationship with Mr. Paul but he didn't let on and when Mr. Paul knocked on his door that afternoon, like any good neighbor, he invited him in. Not much conversation transpired between the two before one-eyed Charlie whacked Mr. Brenton on the back of the head with a blow that "struck him senseless" (*Tragedy Graveyard*). To make it look like he had hit his head on the stove, Charley dragged him over to the wood-burning stove and laid his head against its cast-iron leg. He finished him off by shooting him through the mouth with Brenton's own pistol and left the gun near his hand. It was the perfect crime. The death was classified a suicide and Mr. Brenton was unceremoniously buried in the orchard behind his house. Rumors that Rose and Charley Paul had conspired to eliminate Mr. Brenton made for some stimulating conversation amongst the lake dwellers but after awhile the gossip got stale and discussion turned to other topics.

Rose, now a very young, attractive, "grieving" widow, was truly in need of support but Charley kept his distance at first to avoid further suspicion. When the time was right, he moved in. Charley's scheme had worked. Within a few short months, however, the bloom began fading from the rose as financial pressures put strain on the couple. Rose promised to marry Charley but not until he made enough money to support them both. Fifty dollars a month could keep them afloat, so Charley left to work in a logging camp near Port Angeles. Every payday he faithfully sent his lovely Rose

1924—Indian Citizenship Act declares Indians to be U.S. citizens.

money, and only kept out enough for his room and board.

But life back at the ranch had not improved and Rose was once again feeling lonesome. Her spirits were lifted however, when Mr. Dave McConkey, a bachelor living on the Sol Duc River, heard of her plight and came to the rescue. The two grew fond of each other and eventually Mr. McConkey was invited to stay. Life was good; that is, until Mr. McConkey discovered that Rose was receiving a monthly stipend from her former flame Mr. Paul. He knew that if one-eyed Charley found out Rose had a new roommate, he wouldn't be happy. Refusing Dave's counsel, Rose continued her double-crossing scheme.

Mr. McConkey's warnings should have been heeded. Word eventually reached Mr. Paul that he had a two-timing fiancé. He was furious. He wrote her demanding answers and Rose wrote back telling him not to worry. He was still her one and only. "Someone was just trying to make trouble" (Tragedy Graveyard). Later when the informant named names and advised Mr. Paul that he was being played like a fiddle, Charley became completely unhinged. He immediately wrote her swearing that if she returned his money, he would forget the whole thing. When Rose didn't respond, Paul flew into a rage and fired a letter back, this time threatening that if he did not receive his money by a given date, he would return and kill both her and McConkey.

Realizing he was dealing with a deranged man, Mr. McConkey had a warrant issued for Paul's arrest, to be served by a constable when he landed at Clallam. The boat from Seattle came to Clallam only once a week (on Wednesdays). Apparently Mr. Paul anticipated this action and disembarked at Pysht, one stop before Clallam, and then walked through the woods to keep from being seen by anyone who might know him.

After arriving at his cabin, Mr. Paul picked up a pistol, a shotgun and a hunting knife. He then went to the north side of the lake where his friend Chris lived. Chris was away from home elk hunting. Charley wrote him a note saying that he was borrowing his boat, that Rose had double-crossed him and that he planned to kill her, her lover, and then himself. He also bequeathed Chris his money and his watch.

After leaving the note, Paul made his way to the Brenton home, hid nearby and waited. When Dave McConkey came

out of the outhouse, Charley drew his pistol and shot him in the head, killing him instantly. Rose heard the shot and immediately came running out with a shotgun. Her gun misfired. Fearing for her life, Rose pleaded for forgiveness and begged Charley to sit down, have some breakfast, and discuss the situation. None of this had been her fault. Surely he understood. Maybe they could run away together before the body was discovered. Charley agreed to listen but while eating his eggs and bacon, Rose grabbed a knife from Charley's belt and made a stab at his throat, severely cutting him. They struggled with the knife and after almost severing her fingers prying the knife from her hands, Charley slit her throat.

Conscious that his end was near, Charley took pen and paper from a drawer, wrote a message "to whom it may concern" and described what had taken place. After explaining that his body could be found at his cabin across the lake where he planned to shoot himself, he tacked the blood-stained note on the front door and left. Charley didn't make it home. Instead, halfway across the lake, he ended his agony by shooting himself in the head with his rifle. The boat carrying his body was found later adrift on the lake.

When Chris Grausekrause returned home that day, he read the note Charley had left on his door and immediately rounded up some men to investigate. Recruiting was difficult. Several men refused to join because of Charley's violent reputation. Finally, five men were assembled: Theodore Klahn, Joe Hamilton, August Konopaski, Mr. Crosby and Mr. Terwilliger. None were prepared for the shocking scene they encountered. Mr. McConkey's corpse was found a short distance from the Brenton cabin and as they walked through the doorway, all six men gasped in horror at the sight of Rose's blood-stained body lying motionless on the bed, her raven-black hair matted in blood.

All four victims of this grisly tragedy were buried in a cemetery behind the old Beaver School, subsequently called Tragedy Graveyard for the eleven of fourteen buried here who died violently.

* Mr. Brenton's body was later exhumed and removed to the cemetery behind Beaver School.

Bridging Two Cultures

The Life and Times of the Benevolent Baroness:
Martha Elizabeth Irwin-Merchant-Maybury

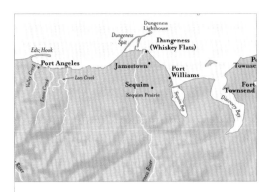

I n a time before the coming of white men to the Olympic Peninsula, in a place near the mouth of the Dungeness River, lived Ste-tee-thlum, a chief of the Klallams. On a very sorrowful day late in his life, the First Wife, "the favored one" of the Ste-tee-thlum, died. The Chief mourned her death bitterly but after an interval began to seek another First Wife. News came to him shortly that the beautiful daughter of a Nanaimo Chief, Princess T'sus-khee-na-kheen, had recently reached womanhood. The old chief was delighted and soon had concocted a scheme to acquire the maiden. Only his favorite son was brought into the conspiracy—a hazardous abduction plan.

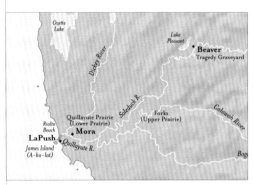

Above: Merchant children, 1891 - shortly after Martha was widowed. Back row: Rose, Ellen, Maude. Front row: Lizzie, Olive, Delphinia   *Rapp Collection*

Previous pages: Young women of Forks Prairie. 1900. Standing second from left - Maude Merchant. Seated from far left: Ellen Merchant, unknown, Olive Merchant, Elma Peterson, Myrtle Peterson, unknown.   *L. White Collection*

Opposite page: Martha Irwin Merchant Maybury. 1880s.   *L. White Collection*

Martha's gold buckle, created from Sam Irwin's finds during the California Gold Rush.

The two of them made the sixty-five mile trip across the Strait of Juan de Fuca and up the east coast of Vancouver Island and by patience and stealth separated the Princess from her keepers. Those accompanying the Princess were sent on their way after being assured that T'sus-khee-na-kheen was being taken for an honorable purpose and not slavery. However, on the return trip to Dungeness the Princess displayed a serious degree of dissatisfaction so that the Chief's son began to think about her plight. At the end of the voyage with expectant Klallam Natives gathered on the beach, the son of Ste-tee-thlum stepped up to his father who was preparing to make an announcement. The son of Ste-tee-thlum spoke: "My father, my honorable, I desire this maiden. Only today I realize I have reached manhood. I would take this daughter of the House of Nanaimo to wife. I am young. She is young. You are old, my father..." Without wavering, the father answered: "I am old. I realize that now. Take the daughter of Nanaimo. Take also my title. Now and from henceforth you shall be known as Chief Ste-tee-thlum the Younger, Chief of all the Klallams." The following day

great merriment, rejoicing and feasting began which lasted many days (Lambert).

Over the years seven sons were born to the new chief and his Nanaimo bride. The seventh son was Lach-ka him who married Qua-tum-a'low. They had eight children, one of whom was Cheech-ma-ham (Chet-ze-moka, "Duke of York") who became chief of all Klallams and friend of white people. (See Introduction) The fourth son of Ste-tee-thlum the Younger was called Ha-que-nilth who married Shu-mal-itsa. The second daughter of Ha-que-nilth and Shu-mal-itsa was called Si-ah-tsa. Si-ah-tsa was born about 1840, was six years old before the British retreated above the 49th parallel, and was ten before the first white settler came to the North Olympic Peninsula. When Si-ah-tsa turned fifteen, the Klallams were still raiding, slavery existed as did the potlatch, and head flattening was still practiced. It is likely that Si-ah-tsa's head had been flattened to show her rank. Only the heads of slaves were left in their natural shape.

About the same year Si-ah-tsa had her puberty dance and feast, smallpox ran rampant (1853) through the Klallam people taking a terrible toll. Si-ah-tsa was a lucky survivor. Equally deadly to the Natives of Dungeness country was B. J. Madison's liquor. For Natives and many whites, whiskey was the crack cocaine of the fifties and sixties, destroying individuals, families, and culture.

Coming to the Sequim Prairie about the same time B.J. Madison set up shop on what became known as Whiskey Flats (Dungeness), was Samuel Sanford Irwin. Sam was born in 1827 in Lawrence County, Alabama and left nine years later eventually making his way to California prior to the Gold Rush. He is listed in the Yuba County, California census of 1850 as a miner. Judging from the amount of real estate Sam acquired and maintained in Clallam County it is clear he did not leave the gold fields empty-handed. On his arrival North Sam filed an initial claim of 320 acres under the Oregon Donation Act. By late fall 1855 Sam was well underway in his farming endeavors. Then came the news of the White River Massacre. In November of 1855 Sam joined Company "I" of the Northern Rangers under the command of Col. Isaac N. Ebey. Sam appears to have been a less than

Si-ah-tsa. Late 1860s. Granddaughter of Klallam Chief Ste-tec-thlum the Younger and mother of Martha Maybury.

1974—February 12th U.S. District Court Judge George Boldt renders his decision against the State of Washington and in favor of Indian Treaty Rights.

Merchant homestead. 1900. Note gramophone on porch.
L. White Collection

enthusiastic soldier, either from his experiences on the battlefield or just as likely from the fact that he had previously caught the eye of a strikingly beautiful Klallam girl. Sam was mustered out February 11, 1856. His respect for the government was diminished further by the fact that Governor Stevens held suspect those whites with Native friends and/or wives, going so far as to issue arrest warrants for several in the late spring of 1856.

So it was that in this time of trouble Samuel Sanford Irwin came to the House of Ha-que-nilth father of Si-ah-tsa seeking her for his wife. They were married in an Indian ceremony and on March 28, 1858, five months before the Indian Wars ended, a bundle of hope was delivered to the homestead cabin of Samuel and Si-ah-tsa Irwin. They called her Martha Elizabeth. Like most children of mixed Klallam/white marriages, Martha was proudly raised culturally as a white child but with a dose of Klallam myth and legend part of her early training. It is also clear from Martha's latter career path that in addition to the usual academic subjects taught by her father, neighbors and later possibly the Sequim School (1868) Martha acquired from her mother and mother's family a working knowledge of local ethnobotany. Martha grew up loving the wide open spaces of Sequim Prairie with its panoramic views of the

Olympics, the Strait and Vancouver Island. She loved the farm animals and loved the family garden but most of all loved the land. However beautiful the landscape, this was still the wild west where justice was swift if not always fair or proportional. Not far from the Irwin farm, in 1864, a "vigilance" committee permanently retired Jack Adams from his rustling business. A few years later a Tsimishan raiding party plucked one of Lame Jack's (Klallam) wives and a son off a Dungeness beach. The Klallam reprisal came September 21, 1868 on Dungeness Spit. Seventeen Tsimishan were killed in their sleep in what has become known as the Dungeness Massacre. White families were terrified by this show of force. It was a force, however, that was fading fast. Over the next several years, disease and alcohol accelerated the Dungeness Klallam unimpeded spiral into oblivion.

In 1873, with the frontier period closing, the new white majority asked for the removal of all Sequim area Natives to the Skokomish Reservation. Death was easier to contemplate. Chief James Balch[1] fought back. In 1874 he pooled the resources of local Natives and bought 210 acres of East Dungeness waterfront property and plotted a townsite known now as Jamestown. James Balch was "mayor," "city attorney" and "police chief." His first order of business was to build a jail for drunks.

Henry Dunning homestead. 1890s.
Located north of Forks down Merchant Road on the Calawah River.
Henry gifted this 160 acre homestead to Martha.
Forks Timber Museum Collection

Trials and Tribulations

Martha Irwin married Ivory Foster Merchant, thirty years her senior, the same year Jamestown was founded by her cousin. The couple began farming at "Groveland" next door to Jamestown on property Sam had purchased to secure a home for his father-in-law, Ha-que-nilth. Martha's siblings, Susan, Ellen, Sam Jr., Matilda and newborn Richard continued to live with their parents on Sequim Prairie where all was not well. Sam had prospered[2] but he had also made enemies. Among other issues, some choked on the idea of a rich Indian neighbor and her half-breed[3] children—after all, there was a law. The 1866 legislation forbade the marriage of white men to women more than one-half blood Indian. On September 14, 1877 a Federal Grand Jury was convened in Port Townsend, Washington Territory. Among those called to testify were friend and neighbor William Waterhouse, son-in-law Ivory Merchant, Dungeness farmer and territorial legislator and Justice of the Peace, Elijah McAlmond, and Superintendent of Clallam County Schools, B.G. Hotchkiss. Sam was indicted for "living in open and notorious fornication with an Indian known as Si-ah-tsa,

Martha's Pharmacy
(From Klallam and Twana Ethnobotany)

Alder	Drink made from inner bark— to purify blood
Blackberry	Roots used for cold remedy
Cedar	Gum chewed for toothache
Cottonwood	Buds used to make eye wash
Crabapple	Bark used to make eye wash
Dogfish Oil	Eyewash for newborns
Fir	Pitch used to close deep cuts
Indian Plum	Leaves chewed by women in labor
Licorice	For colds
Madrona	Syrup from leaves used for throat ailments
Maple	Bark and leaves soaked in water made general tonic
Mussel Shells	Ground and mixed with water used to improve mother's milk production
Nettles	Stalks used to make rubbing compound for stiffness
Oregon grape	Bark and roots used for skin diseases
Potatoes	Scraped and used for burns and scalds
Skunk Cabbage	Leaves used in steam bath for general good health
Spruce	Needles chewed for toothache
Thistle	Roots used to prevent nausea during pregnancy
Wild cherry	Inner bark used in drink for consumption
Wild gooseberry	Inner bark rinse combined with mother's milk used for sore eyes

Above: Martha Maybury, far left, with Forks Prairie women.   L. White Collection

Previous pages: The magnificent Maybury house in Forks. On the ground floor far left was the kitchen; far right behind the porch was the parlor. Between were the living and dining rooms. Martha's table sat twenty. Over it hung a grand chandelier. On the second floor were the girls' bedrooms and behind the bay window, the master bedroom (Martha's room). On the third floor with dormer was the girls' study.   *L. White Collection*

Opposite: Martha Maybury with Wynona Whitcomb, her granddaughter.

Martha's brother, Sam Irwin, and his son, Sam.   *Rapp Collection*

Left: Martha with her grandchildren in Forks. 1910s.

Rapp Collection

Olive and "Bay" Merchant.   *Rupp Collection*

made against the peace and dignity of Washington Territory."
September 15 a warrant was sworn for Sam's arrest which was
served at the Irwin residence September 21 by C. W.
Thompson, Sheriff of Clallam County.

From this blow and its aftermath Sam and Si-ah-tsa did
not recover. Si-ah-tsa did not make her fortieth birthday
and died before the turn of the decade. She was buried on
their Sequim Prairie property, her name written out of
Clallam County history. Martha's sorrow was compounded
during this period by the death in infancy of the only son
she would ever have. Then December 7, 1882, Samuel

Sanford Irwin died leaving Martha 24 years old and
married, Susan 19, and soon to be married, Ellen 17, Sam
Jr. 15, Matilda 11, and Richard, age 9. For thirty years Sam
had given his life and heart to the land and Si-ah-tsa but by
1882 Sequim was a civilized place where independent
frontiersmen and their Native wives were no longer
welcome.

A New Beginning

From the earliest days of her father's trouble Martha's
pioneer spirit sought expression. She was her father's
daughter. The stories brought to her by Bill Waterhouse of
open prairie land on the west side of the Olympic
Peninsula, excited Martha's imagination. In 1881 Ivory
staked a claim to 280 acres between the Ford and Peterson
homesteads on Forks Prairie by marking the couple's future
house site with his green cottonwood walking stick. In 1882
the Merchant family and their belongings were transported
by schooner to LaPush where they boarded canoes for the
trip up the Quillayute and Bogachiel Rivers. On rough and
unsafe stretches of river the women and children were put
ashore. The guide's klootchman carried children Rose and
Maud, and Martha carried baby Ellen through the tangle
along the riverbank. When the Merchant family arrived on
Forks Prairie only one white woman (Esther Ford) and four
white men (Luther Ford, Ely Peterson, Ole Nelson and
Peter Fisher) had come before.

A third family was soon created on the Prairie with the
marriage (Sept. 21, 1882) of Ely Peterson and Winifred Ford,
the sixteen-year-old second daughter of Luther and Esther.
As Martha and Ivory's farm prospered two more girls were
added to the family-Olive and Delphina. During this period
Martha served the needs of the area as midwife and "doctor."
Martha was a diligent practitioner of the healing arts until the
first university trained physician arrived some time after the
turn of the century. Many were the dark nights she left her
protesting husband to attend to a patient in need.

Old friends and family from Sequim occasionally visited
and were welcomed. Sam Jr. stopped by on his freighting
trips to the West End. William Waterhouse brought
newspapers and passable checker games which to a degree,
provided mitigation for his notoriously poor aim when

discarding chew. Martha's ordinarily patient neighbor Esther Ford christened Bill, "Chuckhouse"[4] and their household spittoon the "spit-at." Martha also gained a reputation in those early days for her kindness to strangers. When her house filled with children she put cots on the second floor of the milk-house so she would not have to turn anyone away.

On March 4, 1890 Martha Elizabeth was born and the following year both little Lizzy and her father were stricken with the fever. Lizzy survived. Ivory did not and at age 33 Martha was a widow with six girls to raise and a farm to run. Martha rose to the occasion admirably and in the process caught the attention of Henry Dunning, a bachelor from Vermont. Facts concerning this relationship are scarce and are limited to the surviving letters of one nosy neighbor. It seems that on Dunning's death July 30, 1894, Martha not only inherited the position of second mourner at his graveside memorial, but also was named sole beneficiary of his estate totaling some 160 acres. Martha did not lose any time acquiring another 160 acres in Quillayute/Dickey Country. Her holding now totaled some 600 acres. Martha built impressive dairy barns that were wired with electricity before the town of Forks had power. Her cows were soothed during milking by classical music from a gramophone. Water was diverted from the hillside to minimize cleaning chores.

As progressive as Martha was, the stuff of her nightmares was the automobile and the fear of learning to drive. According to her grandson, Lincoln Sands, Martha's long term solution to this problem was to marry her hired man/driver, William J. Maybury on June 27, 1897. Shortly thereafter the family moved out of their log cabin and into one of the grandest private homes built in Clallam County.

The Most Beautiful Thing

Martha continued her charitable work by founding, with the help of three other ladies, the Congregational Church in Forks, (1903) She donated the land for the church and served as its first secretary. For 23 years she served on the local school board and was a leader in getting phone service to the region. Martha set a standard of service to the community and its institutions that very likely has not been exceeded. She inherited from her father a business mind

and from Si-ah-tsa the generous heart of Klallam royalty. From Si-ah-tsa she learned the social responsibility that comes with wealth and the joy of gifting and of service.

Through her life, in the face of prejudice, bigotry, greed, jealousy and envy, Martha was steadfast in her belief that charity would prevail. To say she was sure of herself in this regard or any other would be an understatement. The family story is told of an argument Martha once had with a daughter over a word's meaning. The daughter referred to a dictionary to prove her point. Martha's dead serious answer pointed out that in this case the dictionary must be wrong! Those who knew her all said the same thing, "Martha was right. Yes, Martha was always right!" It was this single-minded confidence that carried Martha through the events of her life and armored her against the evil in her world.

Wynona Whitcomb, Martha's granddaughter, lived with Martha while she attended school in Forks. Wynona was the first high school graduate of the Forks school system. The following lines are excerpted from the opening of Wynona's graduation speech:

...can you pick one (beautiful thing) that will last longer than an unselfish act of service. A rose or a violet is beautiful but how long will it keep its perfect form and color. A tree is beautiful but eventually its heart will decay and it will fall to the ground. A large well-proportioned building made of marble and granite is beautiful but at last it will become a ruin. A simple act of kindness will outlast them all; will live on through the ages.

These are the words of Wynona Whitcomb but the voice is quintessential Martha Maybury.

The descendents of Martha now number in the hundreds. In these families, around table and hearth, the stories of Sam Irwin, Si-ah-tsa and The House of Ste-tee-thlum are yet told.

---

1. Like Martha, Chief James Balch was a grandchild of Ha-que-nilth.
2. Sam's holdings now totaled over 800 acres.
3. Terminology used in census documents.
4. Chuck means water in Chinook jargon

CHINOOK JARGON: a language used historically by neighboring Northwest coastal tribes.
This collection of words originated from the different tribal languages and later included words from European traders
and European Americans. It was used predominately for trade purposes.

bit—a dime

Boston—an American

ca-nim—a canoe

chuck—water; a river or stream

salt chuck—the sea

cole—cold

cultus—worthless; good for nothing

dol-la—a dollar; money

elite—a slave

halo—none; absent

hee-hee—laughter; amusement

hoh-hoh—to cough

hy-ak—swift, fast

hy-kwa—the shell money of the Pacific Coast

il-la-hie—the grounds; the earth; dirt

in-a-tie—across; opposite to; on the other side

ip-soot—to hide oneself or anything, to keep secret

ik-poo-ie—to shut

kah-kah—a crow

kah-ta—how; why

kal-lak-a-la—a bird

kau-py—coffee

kimtah—behind; after

klah-hanie—out-of-doors

klah-wa—slow, slowly

kla-how-ya—How do you do? Good bye.

klootchman—a woman; a female of any animal

kloshe—good; well

ko-ko—to knock

koo-sah—the sky

kwahta—a quarter of a dollar

kwan-kwan—glad

kwash—fear

la-boo—the mouth; the mouth of a river

la-po-el—a frying pan

moos-moos—buffalo or horned cattle

potlatch—a gift

puss-puss—a cat

sal-lal—the sallal berry

salmon—the salmon

salt—salt or salt taste; salt chuck-the sea

sit-kum—a half; a part

sit-shum—to swim

si-wash—an Indian

skoo-kum—strong; strength

sol-leks—anger; angry

smoke—smoke; clouds; fog; steam

snass—rain; cole snass—snow

te-ah-wit—the leg; the foot

tik-tic—a watch

til-i-kum—people

tuk-wil-la—nuts in general, hazel nut

tum-tum—the heart; the will

tum-wa-ta—a waterfall

tyee—a chief

wa-pa-to—a potato

yi-em—to relate; to tell a story; to confess to a priest;
    story or tale

Archilbald, Lonnie. *There was a Day, Stories of the Pioneers*. Forks, WA: Olympic Graphic Arts, 1999.

Barlow, Elizabeth. Personal interview, 2006.

Beckmann, Darryl. *The Life and Times of Alexander, The man who knows: A Personal Scrapbook*. Rolling Bay, WA. Rolling Bay Press, 1994.

Berton, Pierre. *The Klondike Fever*. New York: Knopf, 1959.

Blackhouse, Frances. *Women of the Klondike*. North Vancouver, B.C.: Whitecap Books, 2000.

Chevigny, Hector. *Russian America: The Great Alaskan Venture, 1741-1867*. Portland: Binford & Mort, 1965.

Clifford, Howard. *The Skagway Story*. Whitehorse, Yukon: Wolfcreek Books, 1975.

Cloud, Dona. "Minerva Troy, Women who made a Difference." Strait History, *Historical Quarterly* of the Clallam County Historical Society and the Museum, Volume 4-No. 2. Port Angeles, WA, 1989.

Dictionary of the Chinook Jargon, or Indian Trade Language of the North Pacific Coast. Victoria, BC: T. N. Hibben & Co., 1889. http://www.1st-hand-history.org/hindex.htm.

Feli, Margaret Elley, *Rivers to Reckon With*. Forks, WA E.C. Gockerell and Craig Fletcher, 1985.

Fish, Harriet Virginia. *Tracks, Trails, and Tales in Clallam County*, State of Washington. Carlsborg, WA. 1983.

Ford, Esther. "The Life of a Civil War Soldiers Wife." Unpublished Memoir. Peterson family archives.

Gorsline, Jerry. *Shadows of Our Ancestors*. Port Townsend, WA. Empty Bowl, 1992.

Gunther, Erna. *Klallam Ethnography*. Seattle: U of W Press, 1927.

Haigh, Jane G. *King Con: The Story of Soapy Smith*. Whitehorse, Yukon, 2006.

Haigh, Jane G. and Claire Rudolf Murphy. *Goldrush Women*. Anchorage, Seattle: Alaska Northwest Books, 1997.

Howe, Sharon. "Women of Clallam County." Strait History, *Historical Quarterly* of the Clallam County Historical Society and the Museum, Volume 8-No. 1. Port Angeles, WA, 1992.

Hult, Ruby E. *The Untamed Olympics*. 3rd ed. Port Angeles, WA: CP Publications, 1989.

Judson, Phoebe Goodell. *A Pioneer's Search for an Ideal Home*. University of Nebraska Press, 1984.

Keeting, Virginia. *Lure of the River*. Port Angeles, WA, 1976.

Kew, Della. *Indian Art and Culture of the Northwest Coast*. Surry, B.C.: Hankcock House, 1974.

Kirk, Ruth. *Exploring Washington's Past: A Road Guide to History*. Seattle: University of Washington Press, 1990.

Klahn. Family Diaries, Unpublished. Forks Memorial Library, Forks, WA.

Lambert, Mary Ann. *The House of the Seven Brothers*. 1960.

Martin, Paul J. *Port Angeles, Washington: a history.* Port Angeles, WA: Peninsula Publishing, 1983.

McDonald, Lucile. *Swan Among the Indians, Life of James G. Swan, 1818-1900.* Portland: Binford & Mort, 1972.

Morgan, Murray. *The Last Wilderness.* New York: Viking Press, 1955.

Morgenroth, Chris. *Footprints in the Olympics, an Autobiography.* Mercer Island, WA: Westwinds Press, 1991.

Olympic Mountain Rescue. *Olympic Mountains, A Climbing Guide.* Seattle, WA, 2006.

Native Peoples of the Olympic Peninsula, Who We Are. Olympic Peninsula Intertribal Cultural Advisory Committee. Norman, Oklahoma: University of Oklahoma Press, 2002.

Owens, Kenneth N. *The Wreck of the Sv. Nikolai.* University of Nebraska Press, 2000.

Pettitt, George A. "The Quileute of La Push, 1775-1945." Anthropological Records Vol. 14, No. 1. Brigham Young University, 1950.

Pilcher, Gilbert. Clallam County Pioneers, "Winifred Ford Peterson's Biography." Port Angeles, WA: Clallam County Museum.

Powell, Jay V. "Quileute Religion and Sites of Religious Importance on the Quileute Reservation at La Push, Washington." Vancouver, B. C., 1981.

Pullen, Royal. "The Pullens... Strong Pioneers at La Push." Strait History. *Historical Quarterly* of the Clallam County Historical Society and the Museum, Vol. 2, No. 4, Port Angeles, WA, 1987.

Ritter, Harry. *Washington's History, The People, Land and Events of the Far Northwest.* Portland, OR, 2003.

Robinson, June. "Laura Hall Peters" Unpublished essay. Clallam County Museum, Port Angeles, WA.

Ruby, Robert H. *Indians of the Pacific Northwest.* Norman, Oklahoma: University of Oklahoma Press, 1981.

Smith, Archer. *Tragedy graveyard, the Starbuck ghost and other true stories.* Forks, WA, 1997.

Smith, LeRoy. *Pioneers of the Olympic Peninsula.* Forks, WA, 1977

Underhill, Ruth. *Indians of the Pacific Northwest.* U.S. Office of Indian Affairs, 1944.

Wahlgren, Iva Hosack. *Memories of a Quileute and Sol Duc Country Pioneer.* Forks, WA, 1956.

Weir, Allen. "Roughing it on Puget Sound in the Early Sixties." The Washington *Historical Quarterly,* Vol. II No 4, 1916.

Whitcomb, Wynona. Graduation Speech. Forks High School. Forks, WA, 1923. Jamestown Library Archive. Sequim, WA.

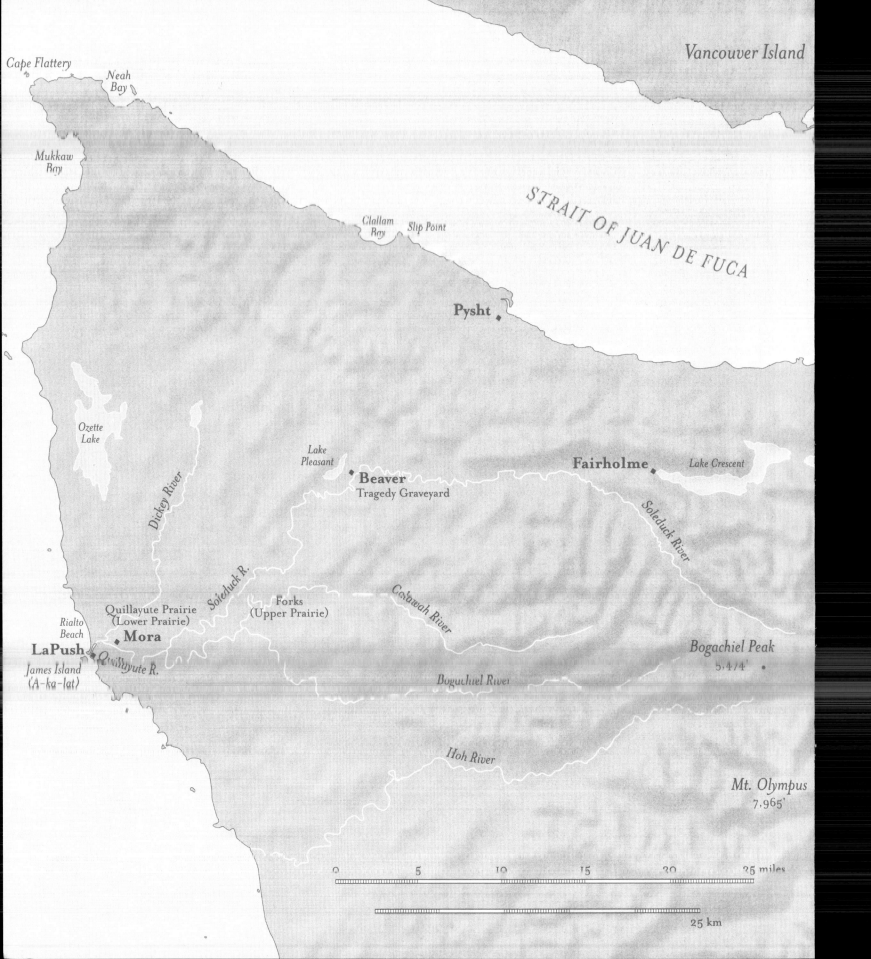

Vancouver Island

Cape Flattery

Neah Bay

Mukkaw Bay

STRAIT OF JUAN DE FUCA

Clallam Bay

Slip Point

Pysht

Ozette Lake

Lake Pleasant

Beaver
Tragedy Graveyard

Fairholme

Lake Crescent

Dickey River

Soleduck River

Soleduck R.

Quillayute Prairie
(Lower Prairie)

Forks
(Upper Prairie)

Calawah River

Rialto Beach

Mora

LaPush

Quillayute R.

James Island
(A-ka-lat)

Bogachiel River

Bogachiel Peak
5,474'

Hoh River

Mt. Olympus
7,965'

0   5   10   15   20   25 miles

25 km